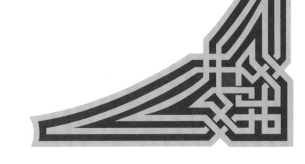

SALAAT
FROM A TO Z

LEARN HOW TO PRAY

A UNIQUE WAY TO LEARN & TEACH SALAAT

Dr. Mamdouh N. Mohamed, All Rights Reserved
www.arabicforeveryone.com

Copyright © 2005,

Windows 9x/ME/2000/NT/XP

بِسْمِ اللَّهِ الرَّحْمَٰنِ الرَّحِيمِ ۝١ الْحَمْدُ لِلَّهِ رَبِّ الْعَالَمِينَ ۝٢ الرَّحْمَٰنِ الرَّحِيمِ ۝٣ مَالِكِ يَوْمِ الدِّينِ ۝٤ إِيَّاكَ نَعْبُدُ وَإِيَّاكَ نَسْتَعِينُ ۝٥ اهْدِنَا الصِّرَاطَ الْمُسْتَقِيمَ ۝٦ صِرَاطَ الَّذِينَ أَنْعَمْتَ عَلَيْهِمْ غَيْرِ الْمَغْضُوبِ عَلَيْهِمْ وَلَا الضَّالِّينَ ۝٧

(see page 99)

Credits

Library of Congress Cataloguing-in-Publication Data
Mamdouh N. Mohamed, Ph.D.
The Islamic Prayer from A to Z
Dr. Mamdouh N. Mohamed
LCCN: 2003094172

p. cm.
Includes references.
ISBN 0-9652877-2-6
Prayer. Islamic prayer. Salat. Salah. Spirituality
Islamic Rituals. Manuals. Guides, Islam, Textbooks, Slide Show, Video on CD.
Worshiping. Instructional books. Religion. Islamic Religion.
How to pray. Handbooks, reference, Fiqh. etc. I Title.
1st Printing 2003 - ISBN 0-9652877-4-2
2nd Printing with CD - ISBN 0-9652877-2-6

Published by B 200 Inc.
10 9 8 7 6 5 4 3

Visit our website at
www.islamfromAtoZ.com

3rd Edition - 2103

 This book contains some photos. Therefore, I found it essential to provide the reader with the fatwaas (rulings) of some well-known scholars on photography.

Ruling on Photography

1) A Fatwaa by Sheikh Ibn 'Uthaymiin

With regard to photography in which the camera captures and produces photographs with no human creation in the image, this is not considered an act of image creation, but it is merely the capture of an image created by Allah the Almighty. The Hadiiths which prohibit image creation refer to those images created by humans to rival Allah's creation. When, for instance, a letter is photocopied, the new copy is not the creation of the machine operator, who in fact might be illiterate, and those who are familiar with the original letter will recognize the copy to be by the same writer. Nevertheless, photography becomes forbidden when used for forbidden purposes. That is, the means to achieve a forbidden matter are also forbidden.

2) A Fatwaa by Sheikh Yusuf al-Qaradaawi

Photographs are basically permissible unless they revolve around forbidden themes such as worship or glorification of photographed objects, especially when this glorified object is one of the people of disbelief such as pagans, deviants and perverted artists.

3) A Fatwaa by Sheikh Abdur-Rahman Abdul-Khaliq

Photographs resemble the reflection of an object in a mirror, and the only difference between the two is that reflections of objects in photographs are permanent while mirror reflections are temporary. Since no one can claim that mirror reflections rival Allah's creation, no one can claim that photographs rival Allah's creation either.

Table of Contents

Table of Contents

Contributors

Salaat
Islamic Prayer From A to Z

I would like to acknowledge those who have contributed to this project
for a great deal of it is owed to them.
The following list does not include all contributors
as some of them did not wish to be acknowledged.
May Allah accept all their good deeds.

NB. The names are not listed in any particular order.

Dr. Eihab Fikri
Dr. Yusuf al-Shibili
Dr. Salah as-Sawi
Br. Abdul Mone'im al-Amin
Sh. Hussam Rifaat
Br. Nadeem Malik
Abdul Moniem, J. Idris
Farooq M. Nihas
Alikaj, Abdul Moneim
Dr. Hussam 'Abdul Hamid
Sister: Yasmin Ali
Sister: Shaimaa Muhammad
Mahdi Mekic
Dr. Ahmad Turkistani
Br. Muhammad al-Shareef
Muhiddin 'Awad Saaleh
Dr. Taj elsir Hamzah
Dr. Fuad al-Ghuneim
Br. Yassir Mohamed
Br. Ashraf Rayhan
Sh. Walid Basuni
Br. Ahmed Merghani
Dr. Ikram al-Haqq
Br. Sulaiman Jalloh
Br. Mohamed, Mohamed
Islam al-Murabit
A. Idris
Ayman Mohamed

Special thanks to the graphic designer:
Bob McDonagh, Innovative Projects

Many others have forfeited their right to acknowledgement seeking
their reward from the Almighty Allah.

May Allah reward all who have made this project possible.

A Washing Both Hands

B Cleaning the Mouth

C Inhaling Water through Nose

D Washing the Face

E Washing Both Arms

F Wiping the Head

G Wiping the Ears

H Washing Both Feet

I Facing the Qiblah

J Takbiirat al-I̱hram

K Reciting the Qur'an

L Making Rukuu'

M Rising from Rukuu'

N Making 1st Sujuud

O Sitting after 1st Sujuud

P Making 2nd Sujuud

Q Rising from Sujuud

R Beginning 2nd Rak'ah

S Making Rukuu'

T Rising from Rukuu'

U Making 1st Sujuud

V Sitting after 1st Sujuud

W Making 2nd Sujuud

X Sitting for Tashah-hud

Y Sitting for Last Tashah-hud

Z Making Tasliim

Section One
General Introductory Issues

Introduction

All praise is to Almighty Allah, who has enabled me to produce this work in its current form. Peace and Blessings of Allah be to our beloved Prophet, Mu<u>h</u>ammad; the final messenger to mankind.

Undoubtedly, everyone in this world strives hard for happiness. This is one of the most commonly sought quality by humans. However, it cannot be attained without purifying one's soul. No matter how hard people try to make themselves happy, without Allah, the Creator of our souls, there can be no guidance on the road to happiness. The Islamic way to attain that happiness is a prescription given by Almighty Allah to humanity. On the top of that prescription is <u>S</u>alaat, which means communication between man and his Lord.

<u>S</u>alaat from A to Z has two main goals:

1. To help every Muslim correct his/her errors and improve the performance of <u>S</u>alaat by using the simple format presented in this book.

2. To help Muslims reconcile fiqh differences by using the Qur'an and the Sun-nah as their references and thus facilitate unity among them.

Authoring a book about such an applied subject is not an easy task. There are hundreds, if not thousands, of books in the Islamic library about this subject in many languages. Each book addresses <u>S</u>alaat from a different perspective. Therefore, to handle this subject from a new perspective was a tremendous challenge for me.

The principal goal of this book is to present <u>S</u>alaat via a how-to-do approach and to explain it in the simplest possible way. As an instructional designer, I explored all possible ways to achieve this goal until I came up with the current format. I hope this guide uplifts Muslims' performance of <u>S</u>alaat.

I also hope that it might be a cause of triggering the love of Allah towards them. It was a kind of challenge to have this book respond to the expectations of many categories: young and old, men and women, Muslims by birth and reverts. Another challenge was how to make a book as a manual and as a reference at the same time; how to present its content in a way that appeals to a culturally diverse audience. Above all, how to filter — from Islam — the various cultural practices of Muslims around the globe.

A third challenge to this project was how to handle the sensitive issue of the ma<u>z</u>aahib. This book examined available proofs cited by many renowned scholars. The approach of the book is impartial. With the help of some well-known scholars, I selected the strongest evidence in the <u>H</u>adiiths of the Messenger (pbuh). Adopting this method has helped me achieve two goals: authenticating the subject matter by relying on the strongest evidence; and avoiding confusion that would have resulted from following different practices of different ma<u>z</u>aahib.

I hope this book will help its audiences perform their daily and other types of <u>S</u>alaats following the model of the Prophet Mu<u>h</u>ammad (pbuh).

In conclusion, I praise the Almighty Allah endlessly for His guidance and ask Him to accept this work.

Dr. Mamdouh N. Mohamed

Who Benefits from This Book

Undoubtedly, the main goal for Muslims in this world is to seek the pleasure of Almighty Allah. Performing S̲alaat is one way to achieve this goal. Therefore, every Muslim must strive for a better level of performance. This book aims to help **every Muslim** achieve this purpose. In brief, it addresses Muslims who are required to perform S̲alaat, i.e., **ten years and older**. This easy-to-read book is mainly designed for such a broad spectrum.

More specifically, this book caters to **new reverts**. They are the second largest target of this book. *S̲alaat: the Islamic Prayer from A to Z* answers their questions. The majority of the available books on the subject lack the needed details that help new reverts perform S̲alaat properly. New converts are also in need of accurate and detailed illustrations to explain issues which are totally new to them. This book provides such illustrations.

The third category includes **teachers, educators, imaams, and parents** who would pass their knowledge to others who, by doing so , bring about changes in society. For these groups as well as for others, the material of this book is based on information derived from authentic and reliable sources. Furthermore, additional readings are provided for those who would like to pursue this particular topic in depth.

Imaams, especially those who work in Western societies, constitute another sector of audience. Hopefully, they would find the book helpful for teaching S̲alaat to new converts/reverts as well as other categories of people. *The Islamic Prayer from A to Z* is designed to be a **textbook**. A three- hour workshop might be adequate to teach "how to perform S̲alaat" at elementary level. Imaams can also use the book for more advanced workshops.

Since many learners raise frequent questions regarding S̲alaat, the book designates large sections to tackle this issue. In these sections the most frequently asked questions by those learners are addressed in a straightforward manner. For more detailed questions, the author refers the reader to a selection of references that can provide more elaborate answers

Although *S̲alaat: the Islamic Prayer from A to Z* is rather comprehensive, it is not meant for students who specialize in Islamic Studies at colleges. Such students require more detailed and more in-depth knowledge. This book, however, can direct them for more research or work at a quick summary of the topic.

The scope of the book is, obviously, very wide. It targets an English speaking audience across the globe regardless of place, culture, or gender. Whatever is presented in Arabic is either a translation of the meanings of verses from the Qur'an or H̲adiith or some terminology that is necessary for understanding the theme, and helps those who are fascinated by Arabic get acquainted with some terminology and expressions used in the literature.

In the last few decades, Islam has become the focal point of the whole world. This book can also benefit the curious and inquisitive non-Muslim reader. *S̲alaat: the Islamic Prayer from A to Z* is made easy and simple for this category which desires to learn more about Islam through genuine sources. This might make the literature a tool to invite **non-Muslims** who have keen interest in Islam.

How to Use This Book

This book consists of 5 sections:

- Section 1 addresses essential introductions for Salaat.
- Section 2 addresses the performance of Ablution (Wuduuˆ)
- Section 3 addresses the performance of Salaat.
- Section 4 addresses other types of Salaat in Islam.
- Section 5 is designated for vital appendices such as supplications, glossary, and references.

Each of the A-to-Z -26 steps has some basic components which guide the audience to access the information they need in no time.

These components are:

1) The name of the step.

2) The **WHAT**, **WHEN**, and **HOW** sections. The WHAT explains what is supposed to be said in that particular step; the WHEN explains the exact timing of the step in terms of time or order among other acts; and the HOW explains the way it should be done.

3) The **EVIDENCE** section presents the proof for these acts from the Qur'an, the Sun-nah, and other sources.

4) The **Q & A** section presents the most frequently asked questions about each particular step.

5) The **COMMON ERRORS** section shows the common mistakes committed by many people in each step.

6) The **GOLDEN TIPS** section is reminds the audience how to maximize the benefit of the Salaat.

7) The **IMAAM & MAˆMUUMS** section is to show the differences between the two different roles.

8) The **MALES & FEMALES** section presents the differences between men and women when performing Salaat.

In fact, using this book effectively depends on the purpose of usage. Therefore, it is necessary to follow these guidelines:

FIRST: If your intention is to learn how to perform Salaat correctly, you need to go through it gradually from the simple to the complex. Therefore, you need to follow this order:

    1) Have a look at *Salat at a Glance* to get a general overview.

    2) Begin looking into *Salat in Steps* to get detailed explanation for every step. It might be unnecessary to read the Q & A section at this phase.

SECOND: If you are an imaam or a teacher, you need to read every step in detail. The evidence section and the Q & A section are of great importance to you.

THIRD: The normal sequence to read the book is to look at the picture at the top of the page, read the name of the step, go through the **WHAT**, **WHEN**, and **HOW** sections, then read the evidence if needed. Finally, read the Q & A section. The rest of the items might be specific. Females definitely need to see this section while moving from one step to another. Pictures are taken from different angles to provide full and precise views of each step.

REMEMBER: whenever you come across a term that you don't understand, check it's meaning in the glossary.

REMEMBER: all Arabic texts are transliterated under section of "What is spoken in Salaat."

Arabic Symbols

^	ء	a	ـَ
th	ث	u	ـُ
<u>h</u>	ح	i	ـِ
kh	خ	aa	ى
<u>z</u>	ذ	aa	ا
<u>s</u>	ص	uu	و
<u>d</u>	ض	ii	ي
<u>t</u>	ط	aw	أو
ż	ظ	ay	أي
،	ع		
gh	غ		
q	ق	Double Letter	ـّ
t	ة		

4

Salaat

A few words from the author

The impact of Salaat is unique.
It captures the heart of any watcher
from the first moment.
The nice postures of the body,
the smooth transition between movements,
the lowering of the eyes to the ground,
the position of the hands on the chest,
and the beauty of Qur'anic recitation manifest
a genuine state of submission, respect, and humbleness
which Muslims show their Lord five times a day.

You can feel it, you can see it, you can touch it.
It is really something amazing.
The pre-Salaat cleaning adds more brightness
to their calm faces.
Undoubtedly,
this Salaat is perfectly designed.
When compared with other religions,
there is nothing like it.
No wonder so many converts
are so deeply touched by the beautiful sight of
Muslims in Salaat.

Praise be to Allah
who perfected everything
in His kingdom.

Dr. Mamdouh N. Mohamed

1) Washing Both Hands

◆ Say: In the name of Allah.
◆ Wash the right hand with the left hand. Then wash the left with the right. (once)

Wuduu at a Glance

2) Rinsing the Mouth

◆ Put some water in the mouth.
◆ Then rinse it.
◆ (3 times)

3) Inhaling Water Through Nose

◆ Inhale the water and blow it off.
◆ (3 times)

4) Washing the Face

◆ From the right ear to the left ear.
◆ From edge of hair to the beard/chin.
◆ (3 times)

5) Washing Both Arms (including elbows)

◆ Wash your right arm with the left hand.
◆ Wash your left arm with the right hand.
◆ (3 times)

6) Wiping the Head

◆ From front to back and back to front.
◆ (Once)

7) Wiping Both Ears

◆ Place the index finger inside the ears and the thumbs outside.
◆ Move the fingers from top to bottom and vice versa (Once).

8) Washing Both Feet

◆ Begin with the right foot.
◆ Wash it including the ankles.
◆ (3 times)

1) Making Takbiir

- Say: Allahu Akbar.

2) Reciting al-Fatiḥah

- Recite al-Fatiḥah.
- Recite a chapter or part of the Qur'an.

3) Making Rukuu'

- Say: Allahu Akbar, while making rukuu'.
- Say: Subḥana rab-biya al-Ażiim
- (3 times)

4) Rising from Rukuu'

- Say: Sami Allahu liman ḥamidah
  Rab-bana wa laka al ḥamd

5) Making 1st Sujuud

- Say: Allahu Akbar, when you prostrate.
- Say: Subḥana rab-biya al-'A'laa
- (3 times)

6) Sitting after 1st Sujuud

- Say: Allahu Akbar, when you sit.
- Say: Rab-bi ighfir lee.
- (2 times)

7) Making 2nd Sujuud

- Say: Allahu Akbar, when you prostrate.
- Say: Subḥana rab-biya al-'A'laa
- (3 times)

8) Rising from 1st Rak'ah

- Stand up, and Say: Allahu Akbar.

16) Making the 2 Tasliimahs

◆ Turn right and say: Assalamu Alaikum wa rahmatu Allah.

◆ Turn left and say: Assalamu Alaikum wa rahmatu Allah

15) Sitting for Reciting Tashah-hud

◆ Sit down, and Recite the whole tashah-hud

14) Making 2nd Sujuud

◆ Say: Allahu Akbar, when you prostrate.

◆ Say: Subhana rab-biya al-'A'laa

◆ (3 times)

13) Sitting after 1st Sujuud

◆ Say: Allahu Akbar, when you sit.

◆ Say: Rab-bi ighfir lee.

◆ (2 times)

12) Making 1st Sujuud

◆ Say: Allahu Akbar, when you prostrate.

◆ Say: Subhana rab-biya al-'A'laa

◆ (3 times)

11) Rising from Rukuu'

◆ Say: Sami' Allahu liman hamidah Rab-bana wa laka al hamd.

10) Making Rukuu'

◆ Say: Allahu Akbar, while making rukuu'.

◆ Say: Subhana rab-biya al-Aẓiim

◆ (3 times)

9) Reciting al-Fatihah

◆ Recite al-Fatihah.

◆ Recite a chapter or part of Qur'an.

The Story of Salaat

The general meaning of Salaat is a supplication from man to the Lord. This meaning implies that Salaat is a connection between man and his Creator. Entering into the state of Salaat simply means establishing a one-to-one communication with Almighty Allah. While in this state, the human being could only say what Allah has prescribed for him to say. The worshipper is licensed only to recite the word of Allah, glorify Him, praise Him, request His aid and seek refuge with Him.

Unlike the other pillars of Islam, Salaat stands unique. It is the only pillar that had been prescribed for Muslims in Heaven, on the Night of the Journey, known as "The Night of Ascension." This shows how significant Salaat is. In the seventh Heaven, Almighty Allah commanded Muhammad (peace be upon him) to perform the FIVE daily Salaats. In fact, this was a great relief from the agonies and the pains which the Messenger Muhammad suffered from before that journey. It was a kind of condolence from the Lord of the universe to His last Messenger (pbuh).

During this great event, Allah spoke directly to His Messenger Muhammad (peace be upon him). He commanded Muhammad (pbuh) to perform 50 daily Salaats. Then, upon advice from the Messenger Moses, the Messenger Muhammad (pbuh) pleaded with Allah for mercy and begged for one reduction after another until the 50 Salaats became only FIVE a day.

This event illustrates how much mercy, love, and compassion Almighty Allah has for the true believers. It also exemplifies the love of Allah for Muhammad (pbuh). For only by his constant appeal to Allah was the number of Salaats reduced from 50 to FIVE. More interestingly, although the daily Salaats are only FIVE, their reward equals that of 50 Salaats. This is one unique quality granted only to the followers of the Messenger Muhammad (pbuh).

Another unique aspect about Salaat is that, while performing it, Muslims all over the world must face only one focal point: the Ka'bah in Makkah. Visualizing this act makes Muslims seem as if they perform Salaat in a tremendous number of circles. The first circle is the smallest and the closest to the Ka'bah while the farthest circle is as large as the whole globe. These circles take the actual shape of the globe which is oval.

It is worth noting that the Ka'bah was the first Salaat direction for mankind. Then, later, Allah commanded people to face al-Masjid al-Aqsa in Jerusalem, in Palestine. When Salaat was first prescribed for the Messenger (pbuh), he used to face al-Masjid al-Aqsa. However, he always had the desire to face the Ka'bah. After some time, Allah granted the Messenger Muhammad (pbuh) his wish and commanded people to face the Ka'bah. Muslims have been facing the Ka'bah ever since.

This quick glimpse exemplifies how essential Salaat is in the lives of Muslims. No wonder that they carefully coach their kids to start performing it as early as the age of seven. It, indeed, nurtures the souls of human beings and connects them with their Lord. It also purifies the heart and mind.

Above all, these FIVE daily Salaats become an irresistible source of tranquility for true believers. Salaat becomes indispensable to them. It eases their lives, comforts their hearts, and connects them with their Lord.

What it Means to be in <u>S</u>alaat

Complete submission to Almighty Allah is the essence of <u>S</u>alaat. The heart, the limbs, the thoughts and the words should fully surrender to Him alone. Therefore, the best time for a Muslim to draw nearer to Allah and to show utmost submission is during <u>S</u>alaat in general and during prostration in particular. This is a golden opportunity for a Muslim to ask for his needs from Almighty Allah.

"The closest moment of a servant to be near to his Lord is when he is in Sujuud." **Muslim**

"أَقْرَبُ ما يَكُونُ الْعَبْدُ مِنْ رَبِّهِ وَهُوَ ساجِدٌ"

One gains more rewards from Almighty Allah when he comes for <u>S</u>alaat with an attentive heart and is fully conscious of his words and actions. Consequently, by the end of <u>S</u>alaat, one is supposed to become a better person as if he has just renewed a contract with his Lord. When one's thoughts are focused on Allah, one's vision in life would be clearer and life would be easier and happier.

When these changes occur, one becomes protected from evil acts and is inclined to do good deeds. As time goes by, one's faith increases while sins decrease. Only in this manner would <u>S</u>alaat be a true barrier between you and the shameful deeds and evil acts.

"Indeed, <u>S</u>alaat restrains from shameful and unjust deeds" **29:45**

﴿ إِنَّ الصَّلاةَ تَنْهَى عَنِ الْفَحْشاءِ وَالْمُنكَرِ ﴾ العنكبوت ٤٥

The more you concentrate, the stronger the connection you establish with God when you are in the state of <u>S</u>alaat. In order to bring <u>S</u>alaat up to this level, one needs to be fully conscious and focused on the <u>S</u>alaat's content. For example, when one recites the Fati<u>h</u>ah, one must remember that one is talking to Allah.

→ **Your Sayings**	**Allah's Responses**
الْحَمْدُ لله رَبّ الْعالَمِين *All praise is due to the lord of the worlds*	حَمَدَني عَبْدي *My servant praised me.*
الرَّحْمنِ الرَّحيمِ *The Most Merciful, the most Compassionate.*	أَثْنَى عَلَيَّ عَبْدي *My servant exalted me.*
مالِكِ يَوْمِ الدِّينِ *The Owner of the Day of Judgment.*	مَجَّدَني عَبْدي *My servant glorified me.*
إِيّاكَ نَعْبُدُ وإِيّاكَ نَسْتَعينُ *You alone we worship, and You alone we seek support from.*	هَذا بَيْني وبَيْنَ عَبْدي نِصْفَيْن - ولِعَبْدي ما سَأَلَ *This is between me and my servant. And he will get what he asked for.*
اهْدِنا الصِّراطَ الْمُسْتَقيمَ صِراطَ الَّذينَ أَنْعَمْتَ عَلَيْهِمْ غَيْرِ الْمَغْضُوبِ عَلَيْهِمْ وَلا الضّالّينَ *Guide us to the straight path. The path of those whom You bestowed your blessings on, not those who deserve Your anger, nor the path of those who are astray.*	هَذا لِعَبْدي ولِعَبْدي ما سَأَلَ *This is between me and my servant. And he will get what he asked for.*

Similarly, tranquility is a key factor in becoming more mindful in <u>S</u>alaat. The Messenger Mu<u>h</u>ammad (pbuh) commanded us not to perform it like a crow which pecks the ground very quickly. When one performs it quickly, one loses concentration and, thus, he or she becomes unaware of what he or she says. <u>S</u>alaat, henceforth, has no effect on the heart and it's benefits are not reaped.

In fact, the Messenger (pbuh) drew the attention of Muslims to the importance of being mindful of what is said in the prayer. He gave them some examples of people who offer <u>S</u>alaats but what is accepted from them might only be its half, third, quarter or even its ninth or tenth. Therefore, he always reminded them that nothing is accepted from one's <u>S</u>alaat except the parts done with full awareness. Once he commanded a man three times to redo his <u>S</u>alaat as it was not done properly because of haste.

"Go back and do it again as you did not perform the <u>S</u>alaat properly." **Agreed upon.**

This <u>h</u>adiith, as well as others, sheds light on how important the issue of perfection is, not only in worship but in every human action as well.

Why Should We Pray?

The unique importance of Salaat is clearly manifested by being obligatory on every sane, adult, male or female Muslim. Without performing the FIVE daily Salaats one cannot be identified as a Muslim. Here are some reasons why we should perform Salaat.

❶ We should pray in response to the command of the Almighty Allah:

"O You who believe! Bow, prostrate, and worship your Lord" **(22:77)**

﴿ يَا أَيُّهَا الَّذِينَ آمَنُوا ارْكَعُوا وَاسْجُدُوا وَاعْبُدُوا رَبَّكُمْ ﴾ الحج ٧٧

❷ Salaat is the main pillar of Islam after the declaration of faith. The Messenger Muhammad (pbuh) explained that by saying:

"Islam is based on five pillars: Declaring that there is no god but Allah and Muhammad is the messenger of Allah; establishing Salaat; paying due Zakaat; fasting Ramadan; and making Pilgrimage for those who are capable of visiting the House." **Agreed upon**

❸ Salaat is an apparent sign of the believers. Almighty Allah said:

"The believers, men and women, are protectors of each other: they enjoin what is just and forbid what is evil: they observe regular Salaat." **(9:71)**

﴿ وَالْمُؤْمِنُونَ وَالْمُؤْمِنَاتُ بَعْضُهُمْ أَوْلِيَاءُ بَعْضٍ يَأْمُرُونَ بِالْمَعْرُوفِ وَيَنْهَوْنَ عَنِ الْمُنْكَرِ وَيُقِيمُونَ الصَّلَاةَ ﴾ التوبة ٧١

❹ Salaat is the essence of 'Ibaadah. The Messenger Muhammad said:

"The best of your deeds is Salaat." **Malik**

" وَخَيْرُ أَعْمَالِكُمُ الصَّلَاةُ "

❺ Salaat is the 1st deed to be judged by Allah on the Day of Judgment. The Messenger Muhammad said:

"The first question that will be addressed to the servant is about Salaat. So, if Salaat is done perfectly, he will be a winner. Otherwise, he will be a loser." **At-Termizi**

" أَوَّلُ مَا يُحَاسَبُ بِهِ الْعَبْدُ يَوْمَ الْقِيَامَةِ الصَّلَاةُ "

❻ Salaat is a very powerful means to sound, guided decisions. Salaat Istikhaarah is basically meant to teach Muslims how to ask Almighty Allah for guidance before making any decision.

❼ Salaat is a strong reminder of Almighty Allah. It is a means that makes Allah love you and honors you.

"Then, do remember Me; I will remember you." **(2:152)**

﴿ فَاذْكُرُونِي أَذْكُرْكُمْ ﴾ البقرة ١٥٢

❽ To show constant need for Allah's guidance and support. Almighty Allah said:

"You alone we worship, and You alone we seek help. Guide us to the straight path." **(1:5-6)**

﴿ إِيَّاكَ نَعْبُدُ وَإِيَّاكَ نَسْتَعِينُ ۝ اهْدِنَا الصِّرَاطَ الْمُسْتَقِيمَ ۝ ﴾ الفاتحة ٥-٦

❾ Consistent performance of Salaat is a sign of true faith. Almighty Allah stated that:

"The Masjids of Allah are frequently visited by those who believed in Allah, and the Last Day; established their prayers; and practice regular Zakaat." **(9:18)**

﴿ إِنَّمَا يَعْمُرُ مَسَاجِدَ اللَّهِ مَنْ آمَنَ بِاللَّهِ وَالْيَوْمِ الْآخِرِ وَأَقَامَ الصَّلَاةَ وَآتَى الزَّكَاةَ ﴾ التوبة ١٨

❿ Salaat is a tool to overcome the agony of ailments and calamities. The Qur'an said:

"O You who believe! Seek help with patience, perseverance, and Salaat. Indeed Allah is with those who are patient." **(2:153)**

﴿ يَا أَيُّهَا الَّذِينَ آمَنُوا اسْتَعِينُوا بِالصَّبْرِ وَالصَّلَاةِ إِنَّ اللَّهَ مَعَ الصَّابِرِينَ ۝ ﴾ البقرة ١٥٣

Fruits of Salaat

Many benefits are gained from Salaat by individuals, communities, nations, and the whole world. Performing Salaat with true devotion would bring about many fruits.

❶ Salaat is a means to purify the souls, the hearts, and the minds from all mental diseases. The Qur'an made it clear:

"Indeed, the winner is the one who purifies (His soul) and glorifies the name of his Lord in Salaat." **(87:14-15)**

﴿ قَـدْ أَفْلَحَ مَن تَزَكَّىٰ ﴿١٤﴾ وَذَكَرَ اسْمَ رَبِّهِ فَصَلَّىٰ ﴿١٥﴾ ﴾ الأعلى ١٤-١٥

❷ Salaat is a means to acquire tranquility, since Salaat is basically a glorification for Almighty Allah.

"Indeed, the hearts gain tranquility by mentioning the name of Allah." **(13:28)**

﴿ أَلَا بِذِكْرِ اللَّهِ تَطْمَئِنُّ الْقُلُوبُ ﴿٢٨﴾ ﴾ الرعد ٢٨

❸ It helps make a person in the company of the Messenger in Paradise. When a companion asked the Messenger Muhammad (pbuh) to ask Allah:

"Let me accompany you in Paradise." Muhammad (pbuh) said: *"Help me by making a lot of sujuuds."*
Muslim

"أَسْأَلُكَ مُرَافَقَتَكَ فِي الْجَنَّةِ - قَالَ: أَعِنِّي عَلَى نَفْسِكَ بِكَثْرَةِ السُّجُودِ"

❹ It is a means of protection from calamities. The Messenger Muhammad (pbuh) said:

"Whoever prays Fajr Salaat will be protected by Allah." **Muslim**

"مَنْ صَلَّى الصُّبْحَ فَهُوَ فِي ذِمَّةِ اللَّهِ"

❺ It is a means to erase sins. "The 5 daily prayers and Friday (Salaat) to Friday (Salaat) are expiation of whatever sins committed between them; as long as major sins are avoided." **Muslim**

"الصَّلَوَاتُ الْخَمْسُ وَالْجُمُعَةُ إِلَى الْجُمُعَةِ مُكَفِّرَاتٌ مَا بَيْنَهُنَّ مَا اجْتُنِبَتِ الْكَبَائِرُ"

❻ It is a cure from fear and panic. The Qur'an said:

"Truly, man was created very impatient. Fretful when the evil touches him. And stingy when the good reaches them except those who pray, those who are consistent in their Salaat" **(70: 19-23)**

﴿ إِنَّ الْإِنسَانَ خُلِقَ هَلُوعًا ﴿١٩﴾ إِذَا مَسَّهُ الشَّرُّ جَزُوعًا ﴿٢٠﴾ وَإِذَا مَسَّهُ الْخَيْرُ مَنُوعًا ﴿٢١﴾ إِلَّا الْمُصَلِّينَ ﴿٢٢﴾ الَّذِينَ هُمْ عَلَى صَلَاتِهِمْ دَائِمُونَ ﴿٢٣﴾ ﴾ المعارج ١٩-٢٣

❼ It is a means of protection from the Hellfire. The Qur'an explained this issue very clearly.

"What dragged you in Hellfire? They will say we were not among those who prayed." **(74:42-43)**

﴿ مَا سَلَكَكُمْ فِي سَقَرَ ﴿٤٢﴾ قَالُوا لَمْ نَكُ مِنَ الْمُصَلِّينَ ﴿٤٣﴾ ﴾ المدثر ٤٢-٤٣

❽ It will mark Muslims with light to be emitted from them on the Day of Judgment.

"On that day, you shall see the believing men and women how their light runs forward before them and by their right hands." **(57:12)**

﴿ يَوْمَ تَرَى الْمُؤْمِنِينَ وَالْمُؤْمِنَاتِ يَسْعَىٰ نُورُهُم بَيْنَ أَيْدِيهِمْ وَبِأَيْمَانِهِم ﴾ الحديد ١٢

❾ True and sincere Salaat protects against committing bad deeds. As a result, the entire society lives in peace and tranquility.

"Certainly, Salaat restrains from shameful and unjust deeds." **(29:45)**

﴿ إِنَّ الصَّلَاةَ تَنْهَىٰ عَنِ الْفَحْشَاءِ وَالْمُنكَرِ ﴾ العنكبوت ٤٥

❿ It leads to success. The call for Salaat emphasizes this five times a day:

"Come to Salaat, Come to Success"

﴿ حَيَّ عَلَى الصَّلَاةِ   حَيَّ عَلَى الْفَلَاحِ ﴾

How the Messenger of Allah Taught the Ṣalaat

The Peace be unto him

"صَلُّوا كما رَأَيْتُمُونِي أُصَلِّي"

"Perform your Salaat as you saw me perform it"

Scholars, by consensus, agree that Ṣalaat is the MAIN pillar of Islam after the declaration of faith. This magnitude makes the accurate performance of Ṣalaat very essential. The only way to perform it correctly is to emulate the best model in his Ṣalaat: the Messenger Muḥammad (peace be unto him). The Messenger himself said: *"Perform your Salat as you saw me performing it."* **Al-Bukhari**

"صَلُّوا كما رَأَيْتُمُونِي أُصَلِّي"

To emphasize the importance of seeing the imam, the Messenger of Allah did not only explain it in words, but, rather in action. He ascended the pulpit, once, while praying then returned to his starting spot. After making the tasliim, he explained that he ascended the pulpit just to let the Muslims watch him do Ṣalaat: i.e., it is permissible, under certain conditions, to move while praying. The ruling was taken from the fact that the Muslims actually saw the Messenger (pbuh) doing it.

"Perform your Ṣalaat as you saw me performing it" has some implications. First, Muslims should follow the Messenger's model alone. In other words, if there is no evidence that the Messenger (pbuh) acted in a certain way, or said something during the Ṣalaat, there is no sense in doing it. If it is mere conjecture, it definitely makes the prayer invalid because the Islamic rule is: *"Indeed conjecture is of no use against the truth."* **(53:28)**

﴿ وَإِنَّ الظَّنَّ لا يُغْنِي مِنَ الْحَقِّ شَيْئًا ﴾ النجم ٢٨

The criterion here is the authenticity of the act or the saying attributed to the Messenger (pbuh). The acts of our parents, friends, teachers and neighbors do not constitute legal evidences if they are not following the acts of the Messenger. What really counts is what the Messenger of Allah did or said or approved. The second issue in the same hadiith is the *seeing* the Messenger (pbuh) perform the Ṣalaat. The actual act of *seeing* is stronger than hearing. This notion made me integrate all these illustrations to make the act of Ṣalaat visible to the eye.

To integrate these pictures and illustrations in the book, I had to collect a group of Fatwaas from scholars across the globe. In the beginning of the book, I listed some Fatwaas of those eminent scholars as a permission for using photos in my book. These Fatwaas helped me make the book become more visual.

Therefore, to perform Ṣalaat properly, Muslims cannot imitate people. Rather, they should follow the footsteps of the Messenger to the level of perfection. This would make everyone comfortable that he or she is doing the correct thing. It is this notion which makes this book urgent.

The Ruling on the Forsaking of Salaat

Because of the great importance of the prayer in Islam, the ruling on one who abandons it should be clear to all Muslims. The Messenger Muhammad (pbuh) made it very clear in many sayings. It is obvious that all these rulings refer to one who intentionally and consistently forsakes the Salaat, not one who forgets it. If the person who forsakes the Salaat does not repent, it becomes a very serious matter. Based upon the Qur'an and the Sun-nah, there is a consensus among scholars that the line between belief and disbelief is the abandonment of Salaat.

"إِنَّ بَيْنَ الرَّجُلِ وَبَيْنَ الشِّرْكِ تَرْكُ الصَّلاةِ"

"Verily, what stands between a human being and disbelief is the abandonment of the prescribed prayer."
Muslim

"العَهْدُ الَّذِي بَيْنَنا وَبَيْنَهُمُ الصَّلاةُ – فَمَنْ تَرَكَها فَقَدْ كَفَرَ"

"The covenant between us and them is the Salaat. Whoever abandons it becomes a disbeliever."
Ahmad & At-Termizi

In any country in the world, a soldier who flees or apostates is conventionally considered a deserter. He is treated as a criminal and a grave punishment is inflicted upon him. Similarly, In Islam, one who intentionally renounces the Salaat becomes subject to various punishments unless he or she repents.

A) Consequences in Life

One who intentionally abandons Salaat is considered as an apostate. Therefore:

- He or she should be separated from spouses.
- After abandoning Salaat, new children are considered illegitimate.
- He or she would be subject to criminal law.
- If one dies, he/she should not be washed.
- Jinaazah (funeral) Salaat should not be performed for them.
- No one should make supplication for them.
- He/she should not be buried with Muslims in the grave yard.
- His wealth is not inherited. It should go to Islamic Treasury.

B) Consequences in the Hereafter

- He/she will not enter paradise.
- Hellfire will be his/her abode.

Certainly, it is the duty of every Muslim to teach each other how serious it is to abandon the Salaat. Therefore, if we see someone neglecting or renouncing the Salaat, we should definitely advise him or her until they repent. When they repent, the above-mentioned consequences become inapplicable, based on the commands of Allah in the Glorious Qur'an: *"So if they repent and establish the Salaat and give the Zakaah, they are your brothers in religion."* **(9:11)**

﴿ فَإِن تَابُوا وَأَقَامُوا الصَّلاةَ وَآتَوُا الزَّكَاةَ فَإِخْوَانُكُمْ فِي الدِّينِ ﴾ **التوبة ١١**

How to Gain Khushuu' in <u>S</u>alaat

What is Khushuu'

Khushuu' during <u>S</u>alaat is misunderstood by some people as crying and weeping. Rather, it is the presence of the heart during an act of 'ibadah. When a person's heart is fully occupied with what he says or hears, he is in a true state of khushuu'. The concept of Khushuu' in <u>S</u>alaat is very essential for the following reasons:

1. It is a vital factor in making a person successful in this life and in the afterlife.

﴿ قَدْ أَفْلَحَ الْمُؤْمِنُونَ ۝ الَّذِينَ هُمْ فِي صَلَاتِهِمْ خَاشِعُونَ ۝ ﴾   المؤمنون ١-٢

"Indeed, the believers, who have khushuu' in their <u>S</u>alaat, are the winners." (23:1-2)

2. It is a contributing factor for the acceptance of <u>S</u>alaat.

3. It is a way to gain more rewards from Almighty Allah; the more khushuu' a person has, the more rewards he gets.

4. Without Khushuu' the heart cannot easily be purified.

Ways to Gain Khushuu'

A) Pre-<u>S</u>alaat

1. A Muslim should know his Lord very well. Knowing whom one worships makes a person a better worshipper. Having clear and authentic knowledge about Allah increases His love in our hearts. Consequently, faith also increases.

2. Avoiding major and minor sins is very helpful in gaining Khushuu', as the heart becomes more receptive to the words of Allah during and after <u>S</u>alaat.

3. Reciting the Qur'an frequently and consistently softens the heart and prepares it for Khushuu'. Hard hearts do not gain Khushuu'.

4. Minimize attachment to worldly matters. Gearing one's intentions towards the Afterlife helps against the temptations of life.

5. Avoid excessive laughter and useless arguments as they harden the heart and lead to heedlessness.

6. Stop working as soon as you hear the A<u>z</u>aan. When you listen attentively to the call of <u>S</u>alaat repeat after the muˆ<u>z</u>-<u>z</u>in then offer the relevant supplication. This prepares you for a smooth transition from the business with worldly matters to the business with <u>S</u>alaat.

7. Performing wuduuˆ immediately after hearing the A<u>z</u>aan prepares you for the pending <u>S</u>alaat. Wuduuˆ also works as a buffer zone before engaging in <u>S</u>alaat.

8. Going to the mosque early for praying and continual mentioning of Allah drives Satan away and helps gain concentration.

9. The waiting time for the congregational <u>S</u>alaat helps create a buffer zone between the state of mind before <u>S</u>alaat and the state during <u>S</u>alaat.

B) During <u>S</u>alaat

1. The Iqaamah itself is a final signal to the mind to be well prepared for performing the actual <u>S</u>alaat. Remember what the messenger of Allah said to Bilal (ra) *"Let us enjoy the comfort of the <u>S</u>alaat."*

2. When you stand facing the Qiblah remember the following:
   a. It might be the last Ṣalaat in your life. There is no guarantee to live longer to catch the next Ṣalaat.

   b. You are standing between the hands of Allah, the Lord of the worlds. How can you be busy with something else?

   c. The angel of death is chasing you.

3. Do not forget to make isti'aẓah. It wards off Satan's whispers.

4. Keep your eyes focused on the place of sujuud. This helps you gain more concentration.

5. When reciting the Fatiḥah, try to recall the response of Allah to you after every ayah you say. (When you say: "al-hamdu lillahi rab-bil 'alamin)", Allah responds: "My servant praised me." etc. This feeling of speaking to Allah puts you in the right mood of khushuu'.

6. Beautifying the recitation of the Qur'an has a positive impact on the heart.

7. Recite the Qur'an slowly and reflect upon its meaning deeply.

8. It is recommended to change the suras that you recite from time to time to avoid the mechanic-like state of repetition.

9. Alternate between the various authentic sunan such as proclaiming a different opening supplication in every Ṣalaat.

10. Undoubtedly, understanding Arabic helps you focus on the intended meaning.

11. Interact with the recited aayahs as this will help you be more focused:
    a. If you hear an ayah about Allah, glorify Him by saying "Subḥaana Allah";

    b. If you hear an ayah about Hellfire, say "a'uuẓu billaahi mina-n-naar".

    c. If you hear a command to make istighfaar, do it.

    d. If you hear an ayah that requests tasbiih, make tasbiih.

12. When you prostrate, remember that this position brings you closer to Allah. Seize the opportunity to make sincere du'aaˆ. Invest these moments in making sincere supplications.

C) Post Ṣalaat

1. When you make tasliim, make istighfaar to Allah as you might have made some errors during Ṣalaat.

2. When you praise Allah, thank Him from the bottom of your heart that you have experienced the beauty of Ṣalaat in your heart. Getting used to this habit prepares you for the next Ṣalaat, as you will always be eager to focus in your prayer.

3. One perfection leads to another perfection. If some one perfects his Ṣalaat once, he would be self-motivated to continue on the same level.

May Allah fill our hearts with khushuu' - Aamen.

One Lord, One Message, One Direction

"Indeed, your nation is one, and I am your Lord, So, worship Me (alone)." (21:92)

Wherever they are on earth, Muslims should direct themselves to the Ka'bah in Makkah, in the Western part of Arabia. In other words, if you are in Europe, you should be facing southeast, in South Africa you should be facing northeast, in Indonesia or Pakistan you should be facing west towards Makkah, in the US you should be facing northeast, and so on.

"Direct yourself towards al-Masjid al-Haraam." (2: 150)

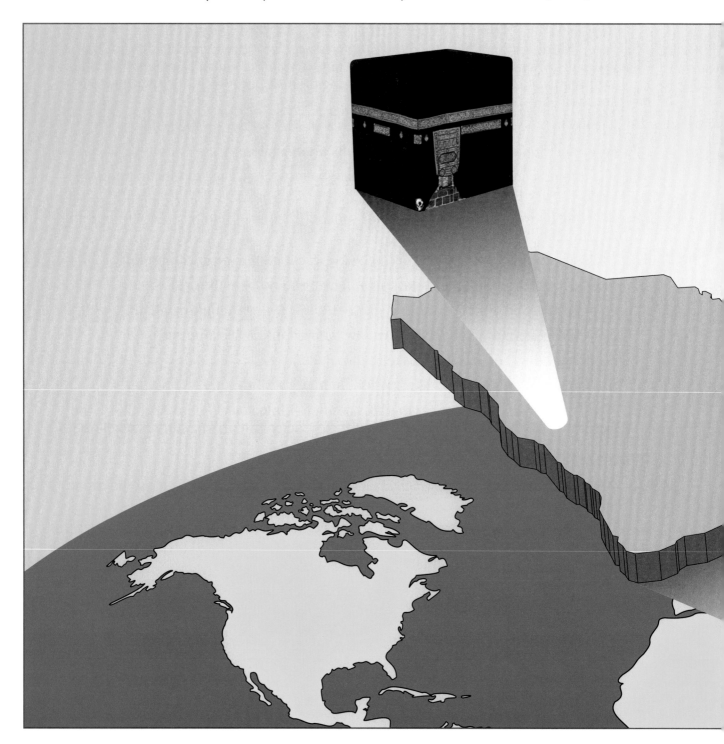

One Lord, One Message, One Direction

﴿ إِنَّ هَذِهِ أُمَّتُكُمْ أُمَّةً وَاحِدَةً وَأَنَا رَبُّكُمْ فَاعْبُدُونِ ﴾ الأنبياء ٩٢

Muslims offer their Salaat at a masjid, a hall, a bedroom, a courtyard, a park, a library, or an airport hall can also work as a prayer room for Muslims. Any of these are suitable for praying so long as they are clean and free of idols. They can also perform their Salaat on an airplane, in a car, on board a ship, or even on horseback.

﴿ فَوَلِّ وَجْهَكَ شَطْرَ الْمَسْجِدِ الْحَرَامِ ﴾ البقرة - ١٥٠

Salaat Times Around the World

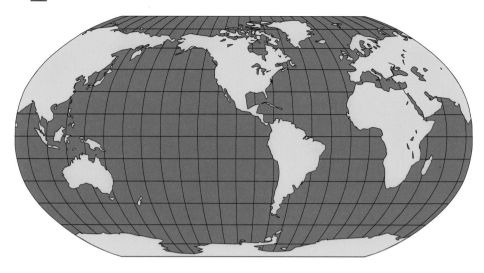

﴾ إِنَّ الصَّلَاةَ كَانَتْ عَلَى الْمُؤْمِنِينَ كِتَابًا مَوْقُوتًا ﴾ النساء ١٠٣

"Indeed, Salaat is an obligation to be performed by the believers in a timely fashion. **(4: 103)**

City	Los Angeles	Washington	Cairo	Makkah	Jerusalem	Baghdad	Cape Town	Cordoba	Istanbul	Moscow
Country	USA	USA	Egypt	K.S.A.	Palestine	Iraq	S. Africa	Spain	Turkey	Russia
Fajr	04:49	04:49	03:46	04:31	04:25	03:44	05:55	05:45	03:18	00:33
Żuhr	12:50	01:05	11:52	12:18	12:36	11:59	12:43	02:16	12:01	11:26
'asr	04:33	04:54	03:29	03:39	04:16	03:31	03:43	06:04	03:53	03:33
Maghrib	07:37	08:00	06:32	06:46	07:19	06:44	06:05	09:09	07:00	07:06
ishaa^	08:52	09:23	07:59	08:05	08:48	08:16	07:30	10:48	08:48	10:26

City	Karachi	Jakarta	Lagos	London	Montreal	Sydney	Auckland	Tehran	Dhaka	Delhi	Manila
Country	Pakistan	Indonesia	Nigeria	U.K.	Canada	Australia	New Zealand	Iran	Bangladesh	India	Philippines
Fajr	04:35	04:42	05:21	03:05	03:44	06:04	06:35	03:38	04:05	04:16	04:19
Żuhr	12:29	11:50	12:44	12:57	12:51	12:52	01:21	12:01	11:56	12:91	11:53
'asr	03:57	03:12	04:00	05:00	04:48	03:52	04:16	03:46	03:21	03:53	03:00
Maghrib	07:01	05:47	06:54	08:22	08:01	06:15	06:39	06:50	06:26	06:57	06:13
ishaa^	08:23	06:58	08:06	10:52	10:00	07:40	08:07	08:25	07:47	08:17	07:28

These times are actual times on May 1st, 2003.

Times of Salaat

﴿ إِنَّ الصَّلَاةَ كَانَتْ عَلَى الْمُؤْمِنِينَ كِتَابًا مَّوْقُوتًا ﴾ النساء ١٠٣

"Indeed, Salaat is an obligation to be performed by the believers in a timely fashion." **(4: 103)**

It is always better to perform Salaat at the early times except for Zuhr Salaat, when the weather is extremely hot and 'ishaa Salaat unless it is not possible.

Warning: There are three times in which Salaat is prohibited.

1. During sunrise
2. During Sunset
3. When the sun reaches its Zenith (Meridian)

The reason for these time restrictions is not to coincide with times observed by the sun worshippers.

Prayer	From	Until	Remarks
Fajr	The beginning of 2nd dawn (the true fajr)	Sunrise	Until the light appears on the horizon from north to south
Żuhr	When the sun declines from its zenith	Objects and their shadows are equal in size	
'asr	From the end of Zhur time	Shadows are twice the size of their objects	In exceptional circumstances, it can be delayed until susnset.
Maghrib	From sunset	The glow of the twilight disappears	
ishaâ	From the end of the twilight	Midnight*	Avoid delaying 'Ishaâ Salaat til after midnight unless you are compelled

*NB. Midnight does not literally mean 12 p.m., it is the mid point between sunset and dawn.

How to Train Your Children to Offer <u>S</u>alaat

Nothing is more valuable than one's own children. We love to see them better than ourselves. One role of parents in this life is to help children maintain the original nature *(fitrah)* in their hearts. To maintain this *fitrah*, we can teach children about their Creator, His names and attributes and how to please Him. Likewise, teaching them the pillars of Islam is another way. Also, training them to perform <u>S</u>alaat is part of maintaining their *fitrah*.

The Messenger Mu<u>h</u>ammad (pbuh) showed the main guidelines to help parents achieve this goal. He said: "Ask your children to perform <u>S</u>alaat at the age of seven and discipline them at the age of ten (if they do not perform it)." In fact, most Muslims observed that if parents miss this golden period, i.e. from 7-10, it takes them a longer time to train their children how to perform prayers regularly.

This hadiith contains the guidelines for coaching children to perform their <u>S</u>alaat: training children to pray begins at the age of seven. Thus, the coaching period should continue for a complete 3 years. This period is adequate for any child to acquire the habit of offering <u>S</u>alaat. To help you coach your children to do this task properly, here are some selected tips:

1. Befriend your children when they are born and maintain this good relationship with them.

2. Teach your children gradually and subtly about their Creator; and how to attribute everything in the universe to Him.

3. Perform voluntary <u>S</u>alaats at home consistently because most children learn by modeling. This also requires the parents to perfect their own <u>S</u>alaat.

4. At the age of 3-5 it becomes natural for children to imitate their parents.

5. If you have older children, let them teach the younger ones how to pray. In general, children like to learn from those who are closer to their own age.

6. Encourage your children to accompany you or your spouse in your <u>S</u>alaat.

7. Motivate your children to join you going to the masjid, if they are able to follow the etiquettes of visiting masjids. If they show more interest, increase the number of their visits to the masjid.

8. Make their visits to the masjids happy experiences. For example, buy them sweets and gifts on their way home. This will reinforce their love of <u>S</u>alaats and mosques.

9. Whenever you enter your house, ask the older children whether or not they performed their <u>S</u>alaats. Make this a habit.

10. Teach your children how to make A<u>z</u>aan and Iqaamah whenever they are capable. Encourage them to make A<u>z</u>aan at home. Children love it very much.

11. Let them join you in Jumu'ah and Eiid <u>S</u>alaats.

12. From time to time ask an adult to perform a voluntary <u>S</u>alaat in front of them. Then ask them to pick up the errors which they noticed.

13. From time to time, awaken your children to make Fajr <u>S</u>alaat, especially on weekends.

14. Train your children to gradually lead <u>S</u>alaat if they know it's rules.

15. Provide them with educational games and software that can help them memorize Qur'an, A<u>z</u>aan, and Du'aaˆ. If these tips are observed, by the age of 10, it becomes natural for children to perform their prayer on a regular basis.

The Importance of Congregational Salaat

Muslims perform Salaat FIVE times a day. These FIVE Salaats fall perfectly within the transitional periods of the day; dawn, noon, afternoon, evening, and night. This distribution helps organize the busy daily life and makes the relationship with the Creator continuous with major focal points during the day.

It is not surprising to see most of the verses in the Qur'an addressing the issue of performing Salaat in the plural form. *"O You who believe! Bow, prostrate, and worship your Lord"* **(22:77)**. In this verse, Almighty Allah commanded the believers to establish the Salaat in congregation, and He emphasized the congregation by saying: "and bow with those who bow." Most verses that talk about Salaat are in the plural form. The importance of the congregational Salaat can be seen in this verse, *"Remember Me (by praying) and I will remember you, and thank me, and do not be ungrateful."* **(2:152)**.

Thus, the Salaat in congregation becomes obligatory for whoever hears the call for Salaat (azaan). One rationale behind praying in congregation is that it makes Salaat easier. Since this obligation is required five times a day throughout life, it might be hard for some people for it requires a strong will and a constant determination. If it were an obligation to be performed individually, it might have been even harder. When in congregation, Salaat becomes easier and more enjoyable, for the concept of equality drives and encourages people. This is very obvious in Ramadan and Friday Salaats.

The second rationale behind praying in congregation is that it strengthens the principle of unity among Muslims. When one performs an act of worship in a group, one naturally develops a sense of brotherhood with others in the same group. The bond among individuals in this group becomes much stronger than the blood tie.

A third rationale is that it fosters the social aspect of the community by helping to build relationships among Muslims from different races and ethnic groups. This leads to visitations, marriages, business and partnerships, all of which translates into a better and more cooperative community.

A fourth wisdom behind the congregational Salaat, and perhaps the most important one is the great reward from Allah. The Messenger explained this in many hadiiths such as *"A man's Salaat in congregation equals 27 folds the Salaat by oneself."*

This is particularly true when we know the following facts:

- A Salaat in al-Aqsaa mosque equals 500 Salaats elsewhere.
- A Salaat at al- Madinah masjid equals 1000 Salaats elsewhere.
- A Salaat in al-Masjid al-Haraam in Makkah equals 100,000 Salaats elsewhere.

A fifth wisdom is that it stresses the concept of equality among people. When the rows are established, we observe that all people stand beside each other: rich and poor, black and white, young and old, ruler and subject. The congregation, therefore, deepens this meaning in the hearts of the believers.

Therefore, it is incumbent upon every Muslim to attend Salaats in congregation. More importantly, it is the duty of Muslims to remind, motivate, and encourage each other to pray in congregations to the best of their abilities. Obviously, Muslims begin coaching their children praying as early as the age of seven.

Recently, it has become common to see some travelers praying in an airport; a team of players offering Salaat in a playground with clothes covering their ('awrahs); a group of people praying in a park, or in a hall. This is a clear manifestation of how important the congregational Salaat is for Muslims. No matter where they are, they should perform it.

Etiquettes of the Masjid

Masjids are the main places for worshiping Allah, the Exalted. They should be kept in the best form and shape. They should help people focus on 'Ibadah and maintain the pure oneness of Allah in the hearts of the believers. Ṣalaat inside mosques which have graves or idols inside prayer halls is not permissible in Islam. Additionally, building a masjid is strongly recommended in Islam. Observing the etiquettes of the masjid also brings about plenty of rewards. Here are some common etiquettes of the masjid:

1. Maintaining the cleanliness of masjids and refreshing them with nice scents.
2. Reciting supplications on your way to masjids.
3. Entering masjids with the right foot while making supplications.
4. Saluting masjids by offering two rak'ahs every time you enter a masjid.
5. Keeping them quiet and calm; lowering voices at masjids.
6. Contributing to the building and maintenance of masjids.
7. Coming to the masjid in the best attire.
8. Reciting the Qur'an at masjids whenever you have time.
9. Helping make masjids a representation of unity among Muslims.
10. Getting to know people in the masjids. (This strengthens the spirit of brotherhood).
11. Avoiding having anything that might hurt others such as coming with a bad smell.
12. Avoiding having any idols or pictures or even distracting decorations.
13. Avoiding playing any type of music at masjids.
14. Avoiding passing in front of people while they are performing Ṣalaats.
15. Avoiding selling and buying inside masjids.
16. Avoiding begging inside masjids.
17. Avoiding co-mixing between males and females.
18. Avoiding any sort of violence or discomfort at masjids.
19. Avoiding arguments inside masjids.
20. Making du'aaˆ while leaving masjids.

Here are some supplications which are part of etiquettes of Masjids:

A Supplication on the way to masjiids

"اللَّهُمَّ اجْعَلْ في قَلْبِي نُوراً- وَفي لِسَانِي نُوراً- واجْعَلْ في سَمْعِي نُوراً – واجْعَلْ في بَصَرِي نُوراً –

واجْعَلْ مِنْ خَلْفِي نُوراً- وَمِنْ أمامي نُوراً – واجْعَلْ مِنْ فَوْقِي نُوراً – وَمِنْ تَحْتِي نُوراً – اللَّهُمَّ أعْطِنِي نُوراً "

"O Allah, place within my heart light, and upon my tongue light, and within my ears light, and within my eyes light, and place behind me light, and in front of me light, and above me light, and beneath me light. O Allah! Bestow upon me light."

A du'aaˆ while entering masjiids

" أعُوذُ بِاللَّهِ العَظِيم وَبِوَجْهِهِ الكَريم وَسُلْطَانِهِ القَديم مِنَ الشَّيْطَانِ الرَّجِيم – اللَّهُمَّ افْتَحْ لِي أبْوابَ رَحْمَتِكَ "

"I take refuge with Allah, the Supreme, and with His Noble Face, and His eternal authority from the accursed devil. In the name of Allah, and prayers and peace be upon Messenger of Allah. O Allah, Open the gates of Your mercy for me."

A du'aaˆ while exiting the masjiids

" بِسْمِ اللَّهِ وَالصَّلاةُ والسَّلامُ عَلَى رَسُولِ اللَّهِ – اللَّهُمَّ إنِّي أسْألُكَ مِنْ فَضْلِكَ – اللَّهُمَّ اعْصِمْنِي مِنَ الشَّيْطَانِ الرَّجِيم "

"In the name of Allah, and prayers and peace be upon the Messenger of Allah. O Allah! I ask You from Your Favour. O Allah! Guard me from the accursed devil!"

A
B Washing Both Hands

C Cleaning the Mouth

D Inhaling Water through Nose

E Washing the Face

F Washing Both Arms

G Wiping the Head

H Wiping the Ears

I Washing Both Feet

J Facing the Qiblah

K Takbiirat al-Ihram

L Reciting the Qur'an

M Making Rukuu'

N Rising from Rukuu'

O Making 1st Sujuud

P Sitting after 1st Sujuud

Q Making 2nd Sujuud

R Rising from Sujuud

S Beginning 2nd Rak'ah

T Making Rukuu'

U Rising from Rukuu'

V Making 1st Sujuud

W Sitting after 1st Sujuud

X Making 2nd Sujuud

Y Sitting for Tashah-hud

Z Sitting for Last Tashah-hud

Making Tasliim

Section Two
Wuduuˆ (Ablution)

Cleanliness الطَّهارَة

Islam pays great attention to cleanliness as it is considered half of one's faith. One of the functions of Salaat is that it cleanses and purifies the heart — the embodiment of one's soul and the most important organ in the human body. Similarly, ghusl (bathing) and wuduuˆ (ablution) are prescribed so as to clean the physical aspect of human beings. Thus, through a perfect Salaat, Muslims can achieve both the spiritual purification as well as the physical cleanliness. In fact, there is a special Salaat to be performed just after the ablution which consists of two rak'ahs (i.e. units).

Acts that require Ghusl:
1. Ejaculation of sperm due to sexual desire.
2. Contact between the genitalia of the husband and the wife.
3. Converting to Islam.
4. Conclusion of the woman's menstruation.
5. Conclusion of post-partum bleeding.

First: Conditions of Major Tahaarah (Ghusl الغُسْلُ)

The conditions of (ghusl) are:

❶	Intention	To intend in one's heart that one is performing wuduuˆ.
❷	Removing what prevents water from covering the limbs	Such as cream, grease, mud, dough, lip stick, paint, fake nails, nail polish, etc.

No.	Step	Ruling
❶	Letting the water touch every part of the body to be washed.	**Rukn**
❷	Saying: *"Bismillah ar-Rahman ar-Raheen"* In the name of Allah the Most Merciful, the Most Compassionate.	**Sun-nah**
❸	Washing the hands 3 times.	**Sun-nah**
❹	Washing the spots covered with impurities.	**Sun-nah**
❺	Performing ablution.	**Sun-nah**
❻	Starting by washing the right side of the body before the left.	**Sun-nah**
❼	Rubbing the body part with water.	**Sun-nah**
❽	Conserving water.	**Sun-nah**

Wuduu^ الوُضوء

Pillars, Obligations and Voluntary Acts of Wuduu^

Conditions of Wuduu^ شُروطُ الوضُوء

There are also two conditions for wuduu^:

❶	Intention	To intend in one's heart that one is performing wuduu^.
❷	Removing what prevents water from covering the limbs	Such as cream, grease, mud, dough, lip stick, paint, fake nails, nail polish, etc.

No.	Step	Ruling
❶	Washing the face including rinsing the mouth and inhaling water through the nose.	**Rukn**
❷	Washing the hands to the elbows (once).	**Rukn**
❸	Wiping the head (once) including the ears.	**Rukn**
❹	Washing the feet including the ankles.	**Rukn**
❺	Performing the steps in order.	**Rukn**
❻	Performing the steps successively with no long interruptions or pauses.	**Rukn**
❼	Saying: *"Bismillahi ar-Rahman ar-Raheem"*	**Sun-nah**
❽	Using a brush (siwaak) during month rinsing.	**Sun-nah**
❾	Washing the hands up to wrists.	**Sun-nah**
❿	Washing parts (limbs) more than once, (except for the head).	**Sun-nah**
⓫	Exaggerating the rinsing of the mouth and the inhaling of water through the nose, (except during fasting).	**Sun-nah**
⓬	Expelling the water from the nose.	
⓭	Starting with the right limb before the left.	**Sun-nah**
⓮	Saying the du'a after wuduu^	**Sun-nah**

" أشْهَدُ انَّ لا إِلَهَ إِلاَّ اللَّهُ وأشْهَدُ انَّ مُحَمَّدًا رَسُولُ اللَّه – اللَّهُمَّ اجْعَلْني مِنَ التَّوَّابِينَ واجْعَلْني مِنَ المُتَطَهِّرِينَ "

What Invalidates the Wuduu^ مُبْطِلاتُ الوضُوء

The issues that invalidate wuduu^:

❶	Natural discharges	Wuduu^ is invalid when urine, stool, gas, blood and anything which comes out of the 2 private parts is discharged.
❷	Sleep	Deep sleep invalidates wuduu^.
❸	Losing one's intellect, conscious or reason	Losing one's mind or reason by ingesting intoxicants, drugs or for any other reason invalidates the wuduu^.
❹	Touching sexual organs with lust	Touching, with bare hands, one's own sexual organs with lust invalidates wuduu^.

Wiping Over Khuf-fain

(socks/shoes/bandage)

المَسْحُ علَى الخُفَّيْنِ

Definition:

It is a case of wuduu^. After one performs wuduu^, one can wear socks. When the wuduu^ is broken, one does not need to take off the socks/shoes/bandage. At the time of wuduu^, one can perform regular wuduu^ except for the feet; he just wipes over them with a wet hand. The wiping should be on the top of socks (not the bottom).

Wiping over bandages, casts, etc.:

1. In case of a bandage, there are no requirements which are observed in wuduu^.
2. There is no specific valid period; it can be used as long as needed.
3. One has to wipe over the **entire** bandage not just part of it.
4. When one with a bandage needs to perform ghusl, one can just wipe over it.

Conditions:

1. The duration of wiping is 24 hours for a resident and 72 hours for a traveler starting from the first time to wipe over the khuf-fain.
2. The khuf-fain should be worn on a state of tahaarah (wuduu^).
3. The khuf-fain should be clean and match the Islamic standards, e.g. from lawful sources.
4. Wiping over the khuf-fain is part of wuduu^, not ghusl.
5. If one wants to make ghusl, he has to take off his socks.

Evidence

❶ Al-Mughirah ibn Shu'bah (ra) narrated that while the Messenger was making wuduu^, *"I tried to take off his khuf-fain. The Messenger said: 'Leave them because when I wore them, my feet were clean (in a state of wuduu^)'"*. **Agreed upon**

❷ 'Ali ibn Abi Talib (ra) said that I saw the Messenger of Allah wiping over the upper part of khuf-fain (not the lower parts)." **Ahmad**

Questions & Answers

Q1 If a person wiped the khuf-fain then he took them off, can he perform Salaat?

A Yes, if he maintains wuduu^.

Q2 What is the ruling on wiping over light, transparent socks?

A It is OK even if the socks have holes in them.

Q3 What is the ruling on wiping over shoes?

A It is permissible to wipe over the shoes (boots) if they cover the feet including the ankles.

Dry Ablution – Tayam-mum التَّيَمُّمُ

Definition of Tayam-mum:

Tayam-mum is a form of dry cleansing. It is done by using earth as a substitute for wuduuˆ and ghusl under the following conditions:

1. When water is unavailable or insufficient.
2. When a person is incapable of using water because of illness or wounds, or because the water is freezing cold and cannot be warmed.

Procedures:

1. Strike both hands lightly on pure earth, rock, or sand.
3. Blow the dust off the hands (optional).
3. Wipe the face once.
4. Wipe the hands (to the wrists) as if you wash them. **Agreed Upon.**

Evidence

❶ 'Am-mar ibn Yassir (ra) narrated that the Messenger of Allah showed them how to make tayam-mum when he placed his hand on the earth. Then he wiped his face and 2 hands.

Questions & Answers

 How long can a person use tayam-mum instead of wuduuˆ?

 He can use tayam-mum as long as he is incapable of using water.

 Should a person renew tayam-mum instead of wuduuˆ?

 No, as long as the person did not break his wuduuˆ. But whenever he is capable of using water, he has to make wuduuˆ.

Washing Both Hands A

Cleaning the Mouth B

Inhaling Water through Nose C

Washing the Face D

Washing Both Arms E

Wiping the Head F

Wiping the Ears G

Washing Both Feet H

Facing the Qiblah I

Takbiirat al-Ihram J

Reciting the Qur'an K

Making Rukuu' L

Rising from Rukuu' M

Wuduu'
from

Z Making Tasliim

Y Sitting for Last Tashah-hud

X Sitting for Tashah-hud

W Making 2nd Sujuud

V Sitting after 1st Sujuud

U Making 1st Sujuud

T Rising from Rukuu'

S Making Rukuu'

R Beginning 2nd Rak'ah

Q Rising from Sujuud

P Making 2nd Sujuud

O Sitting after 1st Sujuud

N Making 1st Sujuud

& Salaat
A to Z

Washing Both Hands

What

◆ Say: بِسْمِ اللَّهِ

"Bismillahi"

Meaning: In the name of Allah.

When

◆ When the intention for wuduuˆ is activated.

How

❶ Wash the right hand with the left one.

❷ Wash the left hand with the right one.

Evidence

❶ *"O You who believe! When you intend to offer Ṣalaat, wash your faces and your hands up to the elbows, wipe your heads, and wash your feet up to the ankles."* **(5: 6)**

❷ On the authority of 'Uthmaan ibn 'Af-faan (ra) that when he performed wuduuˆ he started it by washing his hands 3 times. He then commented on this by saying that: *"He saw the Messenger of Allah (pbuh) perform wuduuˆ in the same manner."* **Agreed upon**

Common Errors

❶ Wasting water.

❷ Not removing paint, ointment, oil, and cream off the hands.

❸ Not washing the left hand due to forgetfulness.

A Golden Tip

❶ Remember that perfection triggers the love of Allah. So, do your best to perfect the act of wuduuˆ as well as all other acts of worship.

"O You who believe! When you intend to offer Ṣalaat, wash your faces and your hands up to the elbows, wipe your heads, and wash your feet up to the ankles." **(5: 6)**

غَسْلُ اليَدَيْنِ

Questions & Answers

1 Q How should one do wuduuˆ if wounded?

A If the washing harms the wound or worsens it, one can use a bandage and wipe over it.

2 Q What if one wears a ring around a finger?

A One can wash the hands without taking the ring off.

3 Q What if a woman has polished nails?

A She should remove the nail polish before wuduuˆ.

4 Q What if a woman wears hinnah on her hands?

A Hinnah usually does not prevent water from reaching the skin. It is permissible to wash the hands even if there is hinnah or any thing that does not prevent water from reaching skin.

5 Q What is the ruling on takhliil (running the water through the fingers)?

A It is the sun-nah of the Messenger of Allah (pbuh).

Imaam, Maˆmuum & Individual

No difference.

Males & Females

No difference.

يَا أَيُّهَا الَّذِينَ آمَنُوا إِذَا قُمْتُمْ إِلَى الصَّلَاةِ فَاغْسِلُوا وُجُوهَكُمْ وَأَيْدِيَكُمْ إِلَى الْمَرَافِقِ وَامْسَحُوا بِرُءُوسِكُمْ وَأَرْجُلَكُمْ إِلَى الْكَعْبَيْنِ ﴿ المائدة ٦

A B C D E F G H I J K L M N O P Q R S T U V W X Y Z

Cleaning the Mouth

What
◆ There is nothing to be said.

When
◆ After washing both hands.

How
1. Take some water into the mouth using the right hand.
2. Rinse your mouth well.
3. Spit the water out , (optional).
4. And do this 3 times.

Evidence
1. The same <u>h</u>adiith of 'Uthmaan ibn 'Af-faan (ra) when he said that he saw the Messenger of Allah (pbuh) rinsing his mouth. **Agreed upon**

Common Errors
1. Not rinsing the mouth properly.
2. Leaving food residue in the mouth.
3. Believing there is a specific du'aaˆ while washing every limb.

A Golden Tip
1. Remember that the mouth and the tongue are guilty of slandering and backbiting. When performing wuduuˆ, recall this and ask Allah to rid you of this sin.

"O You who believe! When you intend to offer Salaat, wash your faces and your hands up to the elbows, wipe your heads, and wash your feet up to the ankles." **(5: 6)**

Questions & Answers

Q1 What if one rinses the mouth once only?

A It is permissible. However, it is better to rinse it 3 times.

Q2 Can one brush one's teeth with a brush while rinsing the mouth?

A It is better to do this before wuduuˆ in order to avoid any interruption.

Q3 Should dentures be removed during wuduu^?

A It is not necessary.

Q4 Is it permissible to speak while performing wuduuˆ?

A Yes.

Q5 How does one rinse the mouth while fasting?

A One can rinse the mouth without exaggeration. This, too, applies to inhaling water through the nose. **Abu Dawuud**

Q6 When performing tayam-mum, should one rinse the mouth?

A No. Nor any part of the body. Only use the earth dust.

Imaam, Maˆmuum & Individual

No difference.

Males & Females

No difference.

يَا أَيُّهَا الَّذِينَ آمَنُوا إِذَا قُمْتُمْ إِلَى الصَّلَاةِ فَاغْسِلُوا وُجُوهَكُمْ وَأَيْدِيَكُمْ إِلَى الْمَرَافِقِ وَامْسَحُوا بِرُءُوسِكُمْ وَأَرْجُلَكُمْ إِلَى الْكَعْبَيْنِ ﴿ المائدة ٦

Inhaling Water through Nose

What
◆ There is nothing to be said.

When
◆ After rinsing the mouth.

How
1. Bring the water to the nose using the right hand.
2. Gently inhale it into the nose.
3. And blow it out using the left hand

Evidence
1. The same hadiith of 'Uthmaan ibn 'Af-faan (ra) when he said that he saw the Messenger of Allah (pbuh) inhale water into his nose. **Agreed upon**

Common Errors
1. Not inhaling the water but letting it touch the nose.

A Golden Tip
1. Remember that when perfecting wuduuˆ, all one's sins fall off just like leaves fall off a tree.

"O You who believe! When you intend to offer Salaat, wash your faces and your hands up to the elbows, wipe your heads, and wash your feet up to the ankles." **(5: 6)**

C

Questions & Answers

Q1 What if one cleans the nose once only?

A It is permissible.

Q2 If a woman wears a nose ring, should she take it off during wuduu^?

A No. She does not have to.

Q3 Is it permissible to rinse the mouth and clean the nose at the same time?

A Yes, it is.

Q4 What if one's nose is wounded and the use of water might be harmful?

A One can let the water just touch the edge of the nose if possible. Otherwise, one can wash all other organs except the nose. Instead of inhaling water into the nose, one can perform tayam-mum.

Imaam, Ma^muum & Individual
No difference.

Males & Females
No difference.

Washing the Face

What
♦ There is nothing to be said.

When
♦ After cleaning the nose.

How
1. Wash the face from the start of the hair line on the forehead to the beard/chin and from ear to ear.

   (3 times)

Evidence
1. Almighty Allah said in the Qur'an: *"O You who believe! When you intend to offer Salaat, wash your faces and your hands up to the elbows, rub your heads, and wash your feet up to the ankles."* **(5: 6)**

Common Errors
1. Not washing the front of the beard due to forgetfulness.

A Golden Tip
1. Prepare for the great Salaat to be performed soon. Do not forget the supplication after finishing wuduu^.

"O You who believe! When you intend to offer Salaat, wash your faces and your hands up to the elbows, wipe your heads, and wash your feet up to the ankles." **(5: 6)**

Questions & Answers

Q 1 What if one forgets to wash the face, what can one do?

A If one remembers this before the end of wuduuˆ, one should go back, wash the face and then do the rest of the parts following the proper sequence.

Q 2 Can a woman wash her face while wearing lip stick?

A If the lip stick is greasy and prevents the water from reaching the skin, she should remove it before washing her face.

Q 3 During wuduuˆ one could have suspicion about having washed the face. What should one do?

A One has to go back, wash the face and continue with the proper sequence.

Q 4 After having finished the wuduuˆ one could have suspicion about having washed the face. What should one do?

A As long as one is uncertain, the wuduuˆ is O.K. But if one is certain, one has to redo the wuduuˆ.

Imaam, Maˆmuum & Individual
No difference.

Males & Females
No difference.

يَا أَيُّهَا الَّذِينَ آمَنُوا إِذَا قُمْتُمْ إِلَى الصَّلَاةِ فَاغْسِلُوا وُجُوهَكُمْ وَأَيْدِيَكُمْ إِلَى الْمَرَافِقِ وَامْسَحُوا بِرُءُوسِكُمْ وَأَرْجُلَكُمْ إِلَى الْكَعْبَيْنِ ۞   المائدة ٦

Washing Both Arms

What

◆ There is nothing to be said.

When

◆ After having finished washing the face.

How

❶ Wash the entire right arm with the left hand.

❷ Wash the entire left arm with the right hand.

❸ And be sure to include the elbows in the washing.

Evidence

❶ Almighty Allah said in the Qur'an: *"O You who believe! When you intend to offer Salaat, wash your faces and your hands up to the elbows, rub your heads, and wash your feet up to the ankles."* **(5: 6)**

❷ Hadiith of 'Uthmaan ibn 'Af-fan (ra). He said, *"I saw the Messenger wash his hands up to the elbows."* **Agreed upon**

Common Errors

❶ Not washing both elbows.

❷ Not rubbing the arms while washing.

A Golden Tip

❶ Islam is the religion of true purity and cleanliness. Always, keep your heart purified and your body clean. The worst heart impurity is to associate others with Allah in worship.

"O You who believe! When you intend to offer Salaat, wash your faces and your hands up to the elbows, wipe your heads, and wash your feet up to the ankles." **(5: 6)**

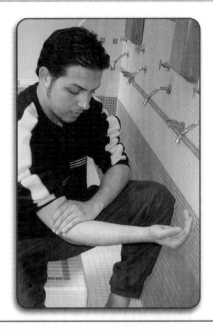

Questions & Answers

1 Q What if one forgets to wash a body part and then remembers it during the Salaat?

A One must break the Salaat immediately and go back to redo the wuduuˆ.

2 Q What if one's arm is bandaged?

A Just wipe on the entire bandage but the uncovered part of the arm has to be washed.

3 Q What if one remembers having washed the left arm before the right one?

A There is no problem. The wuduuˆ is valid.

4 Q Does one need to take off the bracelets before performing the wuduuˆ?

A No. Just be sure that the water runs beneath them. The same rule applies to watches, rings, etc.

Imaam, Maˆmuum & Individual

No difference.

Males & Females

No difference.

يَا أَيُّهَا الَّذِينَ آمَنُوا إِذَا قُمْتُمْ إِلَى الصَّلَاةِ فَاغْسِلُوا وُجُوهَكُمْ وَأَيْدِيَكُمْ إِلَى الْمَرَافِقِ وَامْسَحُوا بِرُءُوسِكُمْ وَأَرْجُلَكُمْ إِلَى الْكَعْبَيْنِ ﴾ المائدة ٦

Wiping the Head

What

◆ There is nothing to be said.

When

◆ After having washed both arms.

How

❶ Wipe the entire head with 2 wet hands.

❷ Begin with the front and end with the back and come forward.

Evidence

❶ Almighty Allah said in the Qur'an: *"O You who believe! When you intend to offer Salaat, wash your faces and your hands up to the elbows, rub your heads, and wash your feet up to the ankles."* **(5: 6)**

Common Errors

❶ Wiping only the front part of the head.

❷ Wiping only the hairy spots.

❸ Wiping the neck.

A Golden Tip

❶ Renew the wuduuˆ whenever possible.

"O You who believe! When you intend to offer Salaat, wash your faces and your hands up to the elbows, wipe your heads, and wash your feet up to the ankles." **(5: 6)**

مَسْحُ الرَّأسِ

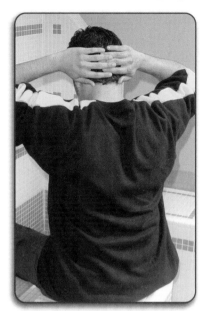

F

Questions & Answers

1 Q What should a bald man do to wipe his head?

A He should start from the original hair line on the forehead even if he does not have hair.

2 Q Some people do not remove from their hair Vaseline, which might prevent the water from reaching the hair. Is it permissible to wipe on it?

A Yes, it is permissible.

3 Q How can a woman with long hair wipe her head?

A She has to wipe over the head only. There is no need to wipe over the entire hair.

4 Q What should a woman do in wuduu^ if her hair is colored?

A It is permissible to wipe over it.

5 Q Can women wipe over their head scarf?

A Yes, provided that she was in a state of wuduu^ when she put the scarf on.

Imaam, Ma^muum & Individual

No difference.

Males

No difference.

Females

Permissable to wipe from front to back only.

يَا أَيُّهَا الَّذِينَ آمَنُوا إِذَا قُمْتُمْ إِلَى الصَّلَاةِ فَاغْسِلُوا وُجُوهَكُمْ وَأَيْدِيَكُمْ إِلَى الْمَرَافِقِ وَامْسَحُوا بِرُءُوسِكُمْ وَأَرْجُلَكُمْ إِلَى الْكَعْبَيْنِ ۞   المائدة ٦

42

Wiping the Ears

What
◆ There is nothing to be said.

When
◆ After having wiped the head.

How
1. Place your index fingers inside the ears and your thumbs outside.
2. Move the fingers from top to bottom and vise versa.

Evidence
1. On the authority of 'Abdullahi Ibn Zaid (ra), who said that he saw the Messenger of Allah (pbuh) wipe his ears with the remaining water which was used to wipe the head. **Muslim**

Common Errors
1. Wipe only the outside of the ear.

A Golden Tip
1. When cleaning the ears, ask yourself: "Do I spiritually clean my ears by keeping them away from listening to forbidden matters?"

"O You who believe! When you intend to offer Salaat, wash your faces and your hands up to the elbows, wipe your heads, and wash your feet up to the ankles." **(5: 6)**

مَسْحُ الأُذُنَيْنِ

  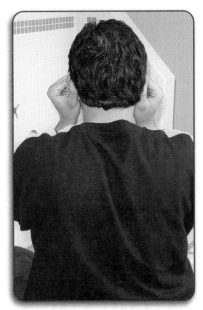

Questions & Answers

Q 1 Should one take off the ear rings when performing wuduuˆ?

A No.

Q 2 In case of tayam-mum, what should one do to the ears?

A Nothing.

Q 3 Should one wipe the ears 3 times?

A Only once is the sun-nah of the Messenger of Allah.

Q 4 If one's ears are wounded and cannot be cleaned with water, what can one do?

A Perform the entire wuduuˆ except the wounded ear(s). After having finished the wuduuˆ make up for wiping the ear by doing a normal tayam-mum.

Imaam, Maˆmuum & Individual

No difference.

Males & Females

No difference.

يَا أَيُّهَا الَّذِينَ آمَنُوا إِذَا قُمْتُمْ إِلَى الصَّلَاةِ فَاغْسِلُوا وُجُوهَكُمْ وَأَيْدِيَكُمْ إِلَى الْمَرَافِقِ وَامْسَحُوا بِرُءُوسِكُمْ وَأَرْجُلَكُمْ إِلَى الْكَعْبَيْنِ ۞ المائدة ٦

Washing Both Feet

What

◆ There is nothing to be said.

◆ After having finished the wuduuˆ, say the famous supplication:

" أَشْهَدُ انَّ لا إِلَهَ إِلاَّ اللَّهُ
وأَشْهَدُ انَّ مُحَمَّدًا رَسُولُ اللَّهِ
اللَّهُمَّ اجْعَلْنِي مِنَ التَّوَّابِينَ
واجْعَلْنِي مِنَ الْمُتَطَهِّرِينَ "

"O Allah let me be among the purified ones and among those who repent."

When

◆ After having washed the ears.

How

❶ Begin with the right foot.

❷ Wash your right foot including the ankles.

❸ And do the same with the left foot.

Evidence

❶ Almighty Allah said in the Qur'an: *"O You who believe! When you intend to offer Salaat, wash your faces and your hands up to the elbows, wipe your heads, and wash your feet up to the ankles."* **(5: 6)**

❷ The hadiith of 'Uthmaan ibn 'Af-faan (ra) when he said: *"That I saw the Messenger Muhammad (pbuh) washing his 2 feet."* **Agreed Upon**

Common Errors

❶ Not including the ankles while washing the feet.

❷ Leaving unwashed spots.

A Golden Tip

❶ Remember that when a Muslim performs wuduuˆ, his sins fall off. It is important to activate this meaning in one's heart and trust the promise of Almighty Allah.

"O You who believe! When you intend to offer Salaat, wash your faces and your hands up to the elbows, wipe your heads, and wash your feet up to the ankles." **(5: 6)**

Questions & Answers

1 Q If after the wuduuˆ one puts on socks then the wuduuˆ breaks can one wipe on the socks?

A Yes.

2 Q Can one wipe on the shoes and wear them while performing Salaat?

A Yes.

3 Q What is the ruling on pouring the water over the feet without rubbing?

A It is permissible. However, rubbing is better.

4 Q Can one dip the feet in a tub of water instead of washing them?

A Yes.

5 Q If one has a missing toe, what can one do?

A One should wash the remaining part of the limb.

6 Q Should one be sitting or standing when performing wuduuˆ?

A Both are permissible.

Imaam, Maˆmuum & Individual
No difference.

Males & Females
No difference.

يَا أَيُّهَا الَّذِينَ آمَنُوا إِذَا قُمْتُمْ إِلَى الصَّلَاةِ فَاغْسِلُوا وُجُوهَكُمْ وَأَيْدِيَكُمْ إِلَى الْمَرَافِقِ وَامْسَحُوا بِرُؤُوسِكُمْ وَأَرْجُلَكُمْ إِلَى الْكَعْبَيْنِ ۞ المائدة ٦

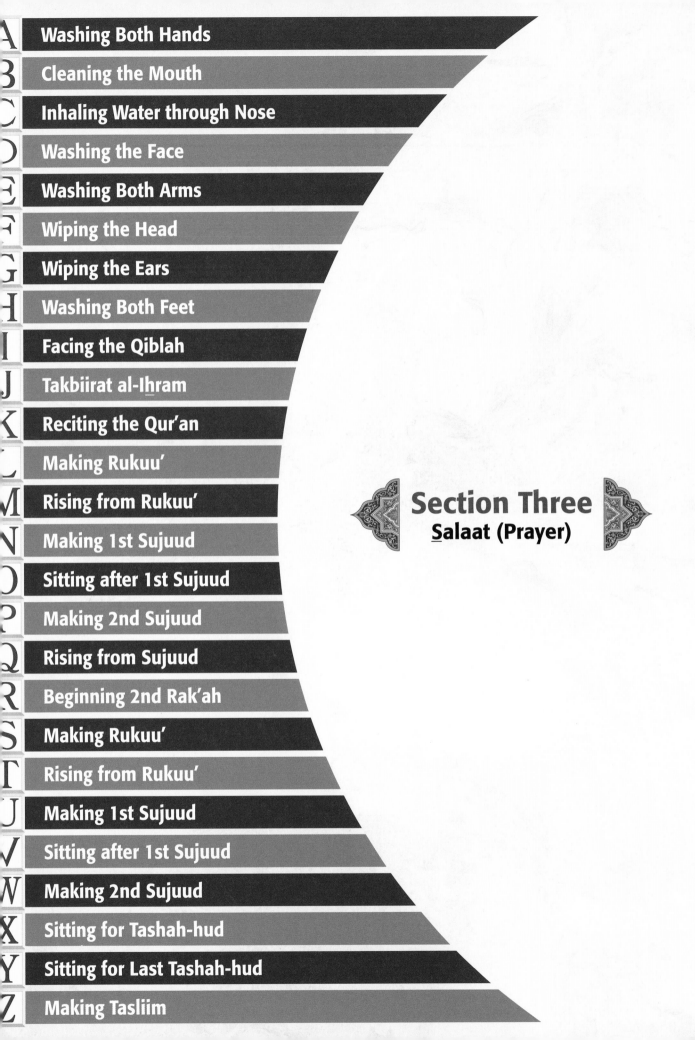

A — Washing Both Hands

B — Cleaning the Mouth

C — Inhaling Water through Nose

D — Washing the Face

E — Washing Both Arms

F — Wiping the Head

G — Wiping the Ears

H — Washing Both Feet

I — Facing the Qiblah

J — Takbiirat al-Ihram

K — Reciting the Qur'an

L — Making Rukuu'

M — Rising from Rukuu'

N — Making 1st Sujuud

O — Sitting after 1st Sujuud

P — Making 2nd Sujuud

Q — Rising from Sujuud

R — Beginning 2nd Rak'ah

S — Making Rukuu'

T — Rising from Rukuu'

U — Making 1st Sujuud

V — Sitting after 1st Sujuud

W — Making 2nd Sujuud

X — Sitting for Tashah-hud

Y — Sitting for Last Tashah-hud

Z — Making Tasliim

Section Three
Salaat (Prayer)

There are also other authentic forms of Azaan.
The following is the most authentic.

Read from right to left.

❶ اللهُ أَكْبَرُ

Allaahu akbar
Allah is Greater

❷ اللهُ أَكْبَرُ

Allaahu akbar
Allah is Greater

❸ أَشْهَدُ أَلاَّ إِلَهَ إِلاَّ اللهُ

Ash-hadu al-la ilaha il-la Allah
I testify that there is no deity
worthy of worship but Allah

❹ أَشْهَدُ أَنَّ مُحَمَّدًا رَسُولُ اللهِ

Ashhadu an-na Muhammadan
rasuulu-l-Allah
I testify that Muhammad
is His messenger

❺ حَيَّ عَلَى الصَّلاةِ

Hay-yaa 'alaa as-salaat
Come to Salaat

❻ حَيَّ عَلَى الفَلاحِ

Hay-yaa 'alaa-l-falaah
Come to Success

❼ الصَّلاةُ خَيْرٌ مِنَ النَّوْمِ

Salaat is better than sleep

❽ اللهُ أَكْبَرُ

Allaahu akbar
Allah is Greater

To perform Azaan correctly follow these steps:

❶ Direct yourself to the Qiblah.
❷ Stick your index fingers in your ears.
❸ Raise your voice to let everyone hear.
❹ Pause after every statement.
❺ Look right when you say statement #5.
❻ Look left when you say statement #6.
❼ Statement #7 is said only at Azaan of Fajr not with any other Azaan.

— Only at Fajr —

❾

لا إِلَهَ إِلاَّ اللهُ

La ilaha il-la Allah
There is no deity worthy of worship but Allah

---

❶ اللهُ أَكْبَرُ

Allaahu akbar
Allah is Greater

❷ اللهُ أَكْبَرُ

Allaahu akbar
Allah is Greater

❸ أَشْهَدُ أَلاَّ إِلَهَ إِلاَّ اللهُ

Ash-hadu al-la ilaha il-la Allah
I testify that there is no deity
worthy of worship but Allah

❹ أَشْهَدُ أَنَّ مُحَمَّدًا رَسُولُ اللهِ

Ashhadu an-na Muhammadan
rasuulu-l-Allah
I testify that Muhammad
is His messenger

❺ حَيَّ عَلَى الصَّلاةِ

Hay-yaa 'alaa as-salaat
Come to Salaat

❻ حَيَّ عَلَى الفَلاحِ

Hay-yaa 'alaa-l-falaah
Come to Success

❼ الصَّلاةُ خَيْرٌ مِنَ النَّوْمِ

Salaat is better than sleep

❽ اللهُ أَكْبَرُ

Allaahu akbar
Allah is Greater

After the Azaan both the Muˆaz-zin and those who heard it should say the following silently:

Peace be unto Muhammad & his family

اللَّهُمَّ صَلِّ وَسَلِّمْ عَلَى مُحَمَّدٍ وَعَلَى آلِ مُحَمَّدٍ

Then a listener says:
O Allah, the Lord of this complete call
and the rising Salaat,
grant Muhammad intercession & merit
and grant him the highest status
which You promised.

اللَّهُمَّ صَلِّ وَسَلِّمْ عَلَى مُحَمَّدٍ وَعَلَى آلِ مُحَمَّدٍ
اللَّهُمَّ رَبَّ هَذِهِ الدَّعْوَةِ التَّامَّةِ وَالصَّلاةِ القَائِمَةِ
آتِ مُحَمَّدًا الوَسِيلَةَ وَالفَضِيلَةَ
وَابْعَثْهُ مَقَامًا مَحْمُودًا الَّذِي وَعَدْتَه

The Call for Iqaamah – (2nd A_zaan)

Although there are other authentic forms of Iqaamah,
here is the most authentic one.

Read from right to left.

❶ اللهُ أَكْبَرُ

Allaahu akbar
Allah is Greater

❶ اللهُ أَكْبَرُ

Allaahu akbar
Allah is Greater

❷ أَشْهَدُ أَنَّ مُحَمَّداً رَسُولُ اللهِ

Ash-hadu an-na Muhammadan
rasuulu-l-Allah
I testify that Mu_hammad
is His messenger

❷ أَشْهَدُ أَلاَّ إِلَهَ إِلاَّ اللهُ

Ash-hadu an-na la ilaha il-la Allah
I testify that there
is no deity but Allah

❸ حَيَّ عَلَى الفَلاحِ

Hay-yaa 'alaa-l-falaah
Come to Success

❸ حَيَّ عَلَى الصَّلاةِ

Hay-yaa 'alaa as-_Salaat
Come to Salaat

❹ قَدْ قامَتِ الصَّلاةُ

Qad qamat as-_Salaat
The Salaat is ready

❹ قَدْ قامَتِ الصَّلاةُ

Qad qaamat as-_Salaat
The Salaat is ready

❺ اللهُ أَكْبَرُ

Allaahu akbar
Allah is Greater

❺ اللهُ أَكْبَرُ

Allaahu akbar
Allah is Greater

❻
لا إِلَهَ إِلاَّ اللهُ
La ilaha il-la Allah
There is no deity worthy of worship but Allah

To perform Iqaamah correctly follow these steps:

❶ Direct yourself to the Qiblah.

❷ Raise your voice to let everyone hear.

❸ Say it faster than the A_zaan.

NB. It is not necessary that the one who calls for A_zaan should be the same one who calls for Iqaamah.

Types of <u>S</u>alaat

Name of <u>S</u>alaat	Ruling
Before Fajr (2)	*****
Fajr <u>S</u>alaat (2)	**Obligatory <u>S</u>alaat**
Duhaa (2+)	***
Before <u>Ż</u>uhr (2) or (4)	*****
<u>Ż</u>uhr <u>S</u>alaat (4)	**Obligatory <u>S</u>alaat**
After <u>Ż</u>uhr (2)	*****
Before 'Asr (2) or (4)	*****
'Asr <u>S</u>alaat (4)	**Obligatory <u>S</u>alaat**
Before Maghrib (2)	***
Maghrib <u>S</u>alaat (3)	**Obligatory <u>S</u>alaat**
After Maghrib (2)	*****
Before Ishaaˆ (2)	***
Ishaaˆ <u>S</u>alaat (4)	**Obligatory <u>S</u>alaat**
After Ishaaˆ (2)	*****
Night <u>S</u>alaat (2+)	***
Witr <u>S</u>alaat (1/3/5/7/9/11)	*****

***** Most Stressed سنن مؤكدة
*** Less Stressed نوافل

There is also an unconditional <u>S</u>alaat which is the 2 rak'ahs to greet a mosque upon entering.

Conditions of Worship

شُرُوطُ العِبادَةِ

It is very essential to know that in any act of worship, two conditions should be fulfilled together. If one is done and the other is ignored, the entire act of worship is invalid.

1. **Sincerity:** worship should be directed only to the Almighty Allah associating no partners with Him.

2. **Correctness:** worship should be done according to the way of the Prophet Muhammad (peace be with him), authenticated with sound evidence to the best knowledge of the performer.

Hence Salaat is a form of worship, it has is own conditions as follows:

Conditions of Salaat

شُرُوطُ الصَّلاةِ

There are 9 conditions for Salaat without which the Salaat is invalid.

◆ The first 3 conditions are general and apply to all acts of worship: Salaat, Fasting, and Pilgrimage.

◆ The remaining 6 conditions are relevant only to Salaat.

Condition	Description
1. Islam	Only a Muslim can perform Salaat. The same Salaat if performed by a non-Muslim is not accepted (by Allah).
2. Sanity	The person should be sane. The insane are not required to perform Salaat.
3. Distinction	The person should have reached the age of distinction (7-10 years old). Before that it does not count.
4. Timing	Salaat is not accepted unless its time is due.
5. General Purity	One's body, clothes and the floor where he/she prays must be cleaned of any impurities before Salaat.
6. Specific Purity	Salaat is not accepted from anyone without wuduuˆ.
7. Covering one's 'awrah	A man should cover the area between the navel and the knees. A woman should cover her entire body except her face and hands.
8. Facing Qiblah	One should face the Qiblah clearly unless it is indiscernible.
9. Intention	One should have a clear intention (in his heart) of which Salaat is being performed.

Pillars, Obligations, Voluntary Acts of Salaat

Rukn رُكْنٌ	Waajib واجِبٌ	Sun-nah سُنَّةٌ

RUKN is any saying or act which, if dropped intentionally, the Salaat becomes invalid but, if forgotten, it must be redone.

WAAJIB is any saying and/or act which, if dropped intentionally, the Salaat becomes invalid but, if forgotten, it can be made up by a special sujuud known as sujuud of sahwu (forgetfulness).

SUN-NAH is any saying or act which, if dropped intentionally, the Salaat is still valid but, if forgotten, no make-up is required.

NB. (Although there are differences of opinion on these issues among scholars, the following are the most authentic).

1.	Praying in a standing position (if capable)	Pillar	رُكْنٌ
2.	Takbiiratu-l-ihraam	Pillar	رُكْنٌ
3.	Raising the hands up to shoulders or up to the ears	Sun-nah	سُنَّةٌ
4.	Opening Supplication	Sun-nah	سُنَّةٌ
5.	Saying: the Isti'aazah	Sun-nah	سُنَّةٌ
6.	Reciting the Fatihah	Pillar	رُكْنٌ
7.	Reciting a suurah or part of it.	Sun-nah	سُنَّةٌ
8.	Announcing takbiir for Rukuu'	Obligation	واجِبٌ
9.	Raising the hands up to the shoulders or the ears	Sun-nah	سُنَّةٌ
10.	Making Rukuu'	Pillar	رُكْنٌ
11.	Saying: "Subhaana rab-biya-l-'Ażiim" (once)	Obligation	واجِبٌ
12.	Saying: "Subhaana rabbiya-l-'Ażiim" (more than once)	Sun-nah	سُنَّةٌ
13.	Rising from Rukuu'	Pillar	رُكْنٌ
14.	Saying: "Sami'a-llaahu liman hamidah" + "rabbana walaka alhamd" For Imaam & Individual: Saying سَمِعَ اللهُ لِمَنْ حَمِدَهُ + رَبَّنَا وَلَكَ الحَمْدُ For Ma^muum: Saying: رَبَّنَا وَلَكَ الحَمْدُ "rabbana walaka alhamd"	Obligation	واجِبٌ
15.	Raising the hands up to the shoulder	Sun-nah	سُنَّةٌ
16.	Saying: حَمْدًا كَثِيرًا طَيِّبًا مُبَارَكًا فِيهِ مِلْءَ السَّمَاوَاتِ وَالأَرْضِ وَمِلْءَ مَا بَيْنَهُمَا وَمِلْءَ مَا شِئْتَ مِنْ شَيْءٍ بَعْدُ	Sun-nah	سُنَّةٌ
17.	Announcing takbiir for sujuud	Obligation	واجِبٌ
18.	Performing the sujuud	Pillar	رُكْنٌ
19.	Saying: (once) سُبْحَانَ رَبِّيَ الأَعْلَى	Obligation	واجِبٌ
20.	Saying: (more than once) سُبْحَانَ رَبِّيَ الأَعْلَى	Sun-nah	سُنَّةٌ

Pillars, Obligations, Voluntary Acts of <u>S</u>alaat

Rukn رُكْنٌ	Waajib وَاجِبٌ	Sun-nah سُنَّةٌ

21. Announcing takbiir to rise from sujuud	Obligation	وَاجِبٌ
24. Sitting after 1st sujuud	Pillar	رُكْنٌ
23. Saying: the du'aaˆ between 2 sujuuds: رَبِّي اغْفِرْ لِي	Sun-nah	سُنَّةٌ
24. Takbiir for the 2nd sujuud	Obligation	وَاجِبٌ
25. Performing the 2nd sujuud	Pillar	رُكْنٌ
26. Saying (once): سُبْحَانَ رَبِّيَ الأَعْلَى	Obligation	وَاجِبٌ
27. Saying (more than once): سُبْحَانَ رَبِّيَ الأَعْلَى	Sun-nah	سُنَّةٌ
28. Performing takbiir for transition to the 2nd rak'ah	Obligation	وَاجِبٌ

This is the end of the 1st rak'ah
For the 2nd rak'ah repeat the above steps.
But instead of standing at the end again you sit for tashah-hud.

29. Sitting for the 1st tashah-hud	Obligation	وَاجِبٌ
30. Reciting the tashahhud	Obligation	وَاجِبٌ
31. Moving your index finger in the tashah-hud	Sun-nah	سُنَّةٌ
32. Sitting on left leg and making the right foot upright	Sun-nah	سُنَّةٌ

The following steps are made is in case of 4 rakat or 3 rakah <u>S</u>alaats

33. Sitting for the 2nd tashah-hud	Pillar	رُكْنٌ
34. Reciting the tashah-hud	Pillar	رُكْنٌ
35. Reciting the salutation (Upon the Prophets)	Pillar	رُكْنٌ
36. Moving your index finger during the tashah-hud	Sun-nah	سُنَّةٌ
37. Sitting on posterior (left buttock), placing the left foot under the right leg and making the right foot upright	Sun-nah	سُنَّةٌ
38. Saying: the du'aaˆ after tashah-hud	Sun-nah	سُنَّةٌ
39. Performing the 1st tasliimah	Pillar	رُكْنٌ
40. Performing the 2nd tasliimah	Sun-nah	سُنَّةٌ
41. Performing steps in order	Pillar	رُكْنٌ
42. Achieving tranquility in every step (not to rush)	Pillar	رُكْنٌ

The sunan are too many to be listed here. But the general rule of sunan is that: whatever is not a rukn or a waajib is considered a sun-nah.

Nullification of Salaat

مُبْطِلاتُ الصَّلاةِ

These are the acts or sayings that invalidate the Salaat.

1. Dropping a condition of Salaat while being capable of doing it, i.e. ignoring the Qiblah direction.
2. Intending to drop a rukn or waajib.
3. Speaking intentionally during Salaat, even few words.
4. Willingly and consciously changing the direction of the Qiblah.
5. Any discharges from either of the 2 private parts (front or back), which invalidates wuduuˆ.
6. Too many unnecessary and uncalled for movements during the Salaat.
7. Loud laughter.
8. Intentional addition of a rukuu' or sujuud to the Salaat.
9. Intentional performance of acts before the Imaam.

Disliked acts in Salaat

مَكْرُوهاتُ الصَّلاةِ

1. All unnecessary movements.
2. Turning the head or looking to the right or to the left.
3. Bringing things that keep people busy such as magazines, newspapers, etc.
4. Putting the hands on one's nipple
6. Raising one's head (or eyes) up to the sky (or ceiling).
6. Closing the eyes during Salaat.
7. Placing the whole arms with elbows on the ground during sujuud.
8. Placing the buttocks between both heels while sitting during tashahud.
9. Interlacing the fingers or crackling the knuckles.
10. Trying to hold or suppress urine or stool during Salaat.
11. Intentionally reciting the Fatihah more than once to get more rewards.

Permissible acts in Salaat

مُباحاتُ الصَّلاةِ

1. Carrying a child during Salaat.
2. Carrying the Qur'an if there is a need.
3. Turning head if there is a need.
4. Responding to a greeting by making a gesture (by slightly raising the hand)
5. Crying while performing Salaat or reciting Qur'an.
6. Correcting the imaam by saying the correct Qur'anic verse.
7. Correcting the imaam by saying subhana Allah.
8. Correcting the imaam by clapping hands (for women).
9. Straightening the rows.
10. Moving some steps to fill a gap in rows.
11. Gently pulling someone to pray beside you.
12. Praising Allah if you sneeze during Salaat.
13. Killing a scorpion, a snake, or any other harmful animal.
14. Turning off mobile phones or any source of disturbance.

Pre-Salaat Checklist

Acts & Words	4	3	2	1
1. I check the cleanliness of my body, clothes, and place of prayer.				
2. After making wuduu^, I offer 2 rak'ahs as sun-nah of wuduu^.				
3. As soon as I hear the Azaan I stop everything I am doing.				
4. I repeat the mu^z-zin's words after every statement.				
5. I make the relevant supplications after Azaan.				
6. I take my children with me to the masjid.				
7. I walk to the masjid with tranquility and respect.				
8. On my way, I urge other Muslims to join me to the masjid.				
9. I offer the du'aa^ upon entering the masjid.				
10. I have time to offer Salaat as salutation to the masjid.				
11. I sit down with the intention to wait for Salaat.				
12. I read some sections from the Qur'an before Salaat.				
13. I stand up for Salaat when the Iqaamah is called.				
14. I do my best to be in the first row.				
15. I straighten my row perfectly by looking right and left.				
16. I leave no gaps between me and people on either side of me.				
17. I remind myself that this Salaat might be my last one.				
18. Before I do Salaat I activate the intention for the Salaat.				
19. I remind myself to observe all the sunan in my Salaat.				
20. I remind myself to make du'aa^ for all Muslims.				

4 = Very strongly   3 = Strongly   2 = Fair   1 = Weak

If you score in this range 70-80 you are excellent.
If you score in this range 50-69 you are fair.
If you score in this range 30-49 you need improvement.
If you score less than 30 you need a lot of work.

TOTAL SCORE

Facing the Qiblah

What

◆ Say: Nothing

Only make the intention in the heart.

When

◆ Right before performing Salaat.

How

In a masjid, look for the mihraab.

Otherwise, use the sun or a compass to locate the Qiblah.

Stand up, direct your face and entire body towards the Qiblah.

Evidence

❶ Almighty Allah said: *"So, direct your face towards al-Masjid al-Haraam, and wherever you (Muslims) are, direct your faces towards it."* **(2: 150)**

❷ *"If the Messenger wanted to pray the obligatory Salaat, he would come down from his she-camel to face the Qiblah."* **Al-Bukhari & Ahmad**

❸ *"The Messenger Muhammad (pbuh) said: "Deeds are indeed judged by intentions and one is rewarded for what one intends."* **Agreed upon**

❹ On the authority of 'mraan Ibn Husain, he said that the Messenger Muhammad (pbuh) said: *"Perform Salaat in a standing position. But if you cannot, pray in a sitting position. But if you cannot, pray on your side. But if you cannot, pray by nodding."* **Al-Bukhari**

Common Errors

❶ Not locating the Qiblah accurately.
❷ Articulating the intention.
❸ Not activating the intention for Salaat.
❹ Wearing transparent clothes during Salaat.
❺ Wearing clothes with photos or pictures on them.

A Golden Tip

❶ Remember, khushuu' does not mean weeping. Rather, it is the presence of mind and heart.

It helps maintain one's focus on Salaat.

"So, direct your face towards al-Masjid al-Haraam, and wherever you (Muslims) are, direct your faces towards it." **2: 150**

اِسْتِقْبالُ القِبْلَةِ

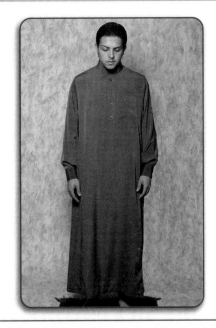

Questions & Answers

Q1 What can one do if one does not know the direction of the Qiblah?

A First, do your best to locate the Qiblah. If you cannot, pray towards any direction.

Q2 What should the ill do when unable to stand during Ṣalaat?

A One can sit. But if this is not possible, one can lie down on one's side.

Q3 Is it permissible to lean on a stick or a pillar during the Ṣalaat?

A Yes, it is if there is a need for it.

Q4 When aboard an airplane or a bus how can one direct oneself to the Qiblah?

A If he cannot determine the Qiblah, one can pray towards any direction.

Q Should I have a sutrah in front of me at every Ṣalaat?

A Yes, but if you don't find a sutrah, you can pray without it.

Imaam
Imaam directs himself towards Qiblah.

Maˆmuum
The maˆmuum does the same.

Individual
The individual does the same.

Males
Direct themselves to Qiblah.

Females
Do the same.

﴿ وَمِنْ حَيْثُ خَرَجْتَ فَوَلِّ وَجْهَكَ شَطْرَ الْمَسْجِدِ الْحَرَامِ وَحَيْثُ مَا كُنْتُمْ فَوَلُّوا وُجُوهَكُمْ شَطْرَهُ ﴾ البقرة –١٥٠

Announcing Takbiirat al-Ihraam

What

◆ Say: " اللَّهُ أَكْبَرُ "

"Allahu Akbar"
Meaning: Allah is Greater

When

◆ After having faced the Qiblah.

How

While announcing takbiir,

❶ Raise the hands parallel to the shoulders or close to the lower ends of the ears.

❷ Keep the eyes on the place of sujuud.

Evidence

❶ The Messenger Muhammad (pbuh) said: *"If you stand up for Salaat, perfect your ablution, then face the Qiblah and announce takbiir."* **Al-Bukhari & Muslim**

❷ In other hadiiths, the Messenger of Allah (pbuh) used to raise his hands while announcing takbiir; and sometimes before takbiir, and some other times even after takbiir. **Muslim & Abu Dawuud**

Common Errors

❶ Raising the hands only as high as the chest or belly.
❷ Raising the head up to the sky or ceiling.
❸ Announcing takbiir while the body is not upright.
❹ Touching the earlobes.
❺ Prolonging the word Akbar (Akbaar).

A Golden Tip

❶ Remember that whoever attends Salaat in congregation without missing the first takbiir, he will be granted two kinds of protections: a protection from hellfire and a protection from hypocrisy. **Al-Termizi**

"Indeed whosoever purifies himself shall achieve success, and remembers the Name of his Lord, and prays." **87: 14-15**

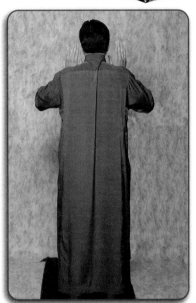

Questions & Answers

Q1 If one catches up with the imaam during rukuu', can one announce takbiir while in the position of rukuu'?

A No, it is not permissible. One has to announce takbiir while standing and before initiating Rukuu'.

Q2 Can we replace "Allahu Akbar" with any other statement inside Salaat?

A No, because the Messenger (pbuh) only said Allahu Akbar.

Q3 Does the Salaat become invalid if one announces takbiir without raising the hands?

A No, Raising the hands is a sun-nah and does not invalidate the Salaat.

Q4 Does a woman raise her hands up to her shoulders?

A Yes, unless this might uncover parts of her body.

Imaam
The imaam raises his voice.

Ma^muum
The ma^muum does not.

Individual
The individual does not.

Males
No difference.

Females
No difference.

قَدْ أَفْلَحَ مَن تَزَكَّىٰ ﴿١٤﴾ وَذَكَرَ اسْمَ رَبِّهِ فَصَلَّىٰ ﴿١٥﴾ الأعلى ١٤-١٥

Reciting the Qur'an

What

◆ Say:

" سُبْحانَكَ اللَّهُمَّ وَبِحَمْدِكَ
وَتَبارَكَ اسْمَكَ وَتعالَى
جَدُّكَ ولا إِلَهَ غَيْرُكَ "

◆ Say: A'uzuu billahi mina ash-shaitani ar-rajiim silently.

◆ Say: bismillahi ar-Rahman ar-Rahim silently.

◆ Recite al-Fatihah.

◆ Recite any surah or part of it.

When

◆ After finishing the takbiir, place the hands on the chest.

How

❶ Begin reciting the opening supplication silently.

❷ Say isti'azah silently.

❸ Say bismillahi ar-Rahmaan ar-Rahiim silently.

❹ Recite al-Fatihah aloud.

❺ Recite a surah or part of it aloud.

❻ Look at the place of sujuud.

❼ Place the hands on the chest: the right hand on the left.

Evidence

❶ 'Aishaa (ra) narrated that the Messenger Muhammad (peace be upon him) used to recite an opening supplication such as *"Subhanaka Allahu wa bihamdika wa tabaraka ismuka wa ta'aala jad-duka, wa la ilaha ghairuk."* **Abu Dawuud & At-Termizi**

❷ Saying the isti'azah as the Qur'an commanded: *"Whenever you read the Qur'an take refuge with Allah from Satan, the Accursed one."* **(16: 98)**

❸ Reading the Fatiha is a must unless one is incapable. On the authority of 'ubadah ibn as-Samet, he said that the messenger of Allah (pbuh) said: *"The Salaat is invalid for whom who does recite umm al-Qur'an (al-Fatihah)."* **Agreed upon**

❹ The Messenger Muhammad (pbuh) said that: *"If the imaam says Amen, you say Amen."*

❺ The Messenger Muhammad (pbuh) Mu'aaz ibn Jabel by saying: *"If you lead people in a Salaat, read (surah) (Wash-shamsi wa duhaha), and (Sabbih isma rabbika al-A'laa); and surah (Iqraˆ bsimi rab_bika) and surah (Wallaili izaa yaghsha)."* **Agreed upon**

Common Errors

❶ Saying isti'azah aloud.

❷ Not saying the basmalah.

❸ Not perfecting the recitation of al-Fatihah.

❹ Not saying Amen.

❺ Turning the face away from the place of sujuud.

A Golden Tip

❶ Remember that Allah is communicating with you. He is responding to every verse you say in al-Fatihah. To benefit from your Salaat, you should have a present heart.

"So, recite you of the Qur'an as much as may be easy for you." **73: 20**

قِرَاءَةُ القُرْآنِ

Questions & Answers

1 What if one says basmalah aloud?

One should not object to it. There are some narrations that the Messenger Muhammad (peace be upon him) said it aloud.

2 What if one forgets to say the opening supplication?

The Salaat is valid.

3 What if one does not memorize the Fatihah?

One can make tasbiih and tahmiid instead.

4 Should the maˆmuum read the Fatihah?

The strongest opinion among scholars is that one should, even if the imaam does not pause after his recitation.

5 Can the imaam or the individual recite the same surah in 2 successive rak'ahs?

Yes.

6 Is it permissible to recite the Fatihah or any Qur'an or zikr without moving the lips and tongue?

No. One has to move the lips and tongue whether an imaam or maˆmuum.

Imaam
The imaam recites al-Fatihah & Qur'an aloud.

Maˆmuum
The maˆmuum reads al-Fatihah silently.

Individual
The individual reads it silently.

Males
Raise their voices when saying: "Amen".

Females
Do not.

﴿ فَاقْرَءُوا مَا تَيَسَّرَ مِنَ القُرْآنِ ﴾ المزمل ٢٠

Making Rukuu'

What

◆ Say: " اللَّهُ أَكْبَرُ "

"Allahu Akbar"
Meaning: Allah is Greater

◆ Bow and say:

" سُبْحانَ رَبِّيَ العَظيمِ "

"Subhana rab-biya al-'Ażiim"

Meaning: Glory be to my
Lord, the Greatest.

When

◆ After having recited the Qur'an, announce takbiir for rukuu'.

How

While announcing takbiir,

1 Raise the hands as in the 1st takbiir.

2 Bow down while announcing takbiir.

3 Both the head and the back should be parallel to the ground.

4 Place the hands on the knees. Spread the fingers.

5 Look at the place of sujuud.

Evidence

1 The Messenger Muhammad (pbuh) said: *"If you bow, place the palms on the knees, spread the fingers and remain still until every limb rests into its position."* **Ibn Hib-ban**

2 When the verse (Sab-bihi isma rab-bika Al-Ażiim) was revealed, the Messenger Muhammad said: *"say it while doing rukuu'."* **Ahmad, Abu-Dawuud, and Ibn Majah**

Common Errors

1 Not straightening the back.

2 Not looking at the place of sujuud.

3 Not placing the hands on the knees.

4 Rushing the rukuu'.

A Golden Tip

1 Bowing is a clear sign of submission. So, remember the one for whom you are bowing. This will help you gain more khushuu'.

"And perform as-Salaat, and give Zakaat, and bow down with obedience to Allah, along with ar-Raki'iin." **2: 43**

الرُّكُوعُ

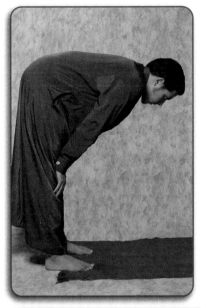  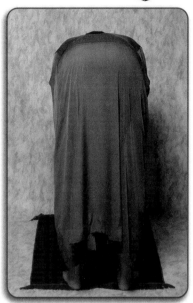

Questions & Answers

Q 1 What if one initiates the rukuu' before the imaam?

A If done intentionally, the Salaat is invalid. But if done inadvertently, one should wait in the same position until the imaam reaches there. The maˆmuum should always follow the imaam.

Q 2 Is it enough to say: (Subhana rab-biya al-'Ażiim) once, or should it be said more?

A Once is enough. But saying it more than once is a sun-nah which will render more rewards.

Q 3 If one catches up with the imaam in rukuu', does one announce one takbiir or two?

A One can announce one takbiir with the intention to include both takbirat al-Ihraam and ar-rukuu'. One can also announce two takbiirs.

Q 4 What should the tardy maˆmuum do when initiating the rukuu' as the imaam immediately rises from rukuu'?

A One should say: (Subhana rab-biya al-Ażiim) even if the imaam rises from rukuu'.

Q 5 If the tardy maˆmuum catches up with the imaam during the rukuu', does the maˆmuum's rukuu' count as a full rak'ah?

A Yes, if the maˆmuum does not miss the rukuu' with the imaam. The maˆmuum does not have to recite the Fatihah and does not need to make up for a whole rak'ah.

Imaam
The imaam raises his voice when announcing takbiir.

Maˆmuum
The maˆmuum does not.

Individual
The individual does not.

Males
No difference.

Females
No difference.

﴿ وَأَقِيمُوا الصَّلَاةَ وَآتُوا الزَّكَاةَ وَارْكَعُوا مَعَ الرَّاكِعِينَ ﴾ البقرة ٤٣

What

◆ While rising to the upright position, the imaam and the individual should say:

" سَمِعَ اللَّهُ لِمَنْ حَمِدَهُ "

◆ "Sami'a Allahu liman hamidah."

◆ Then all of them should say:

" رَبَّنا وَلَكَ الحَمْدُ "

◆ "Rab-bana walaka al-hamd" (silently).

When

◆ After having finished rukuu'.

How

❶ Raise the upper body back to its upright position.

❷ Raise the hands parallel to the shoulder or to the lower ends of the ears.

❸ Place the hands on the chest: the right hand on the left.

❹ Keep the eyes on the place of sujuud.

Evidence

❶ The Messenger Muhammad (pbuh) advised the person who did not perform his Salaat well: *"Then say: "Sami'a Allahu liman hamidah. Then stand still."* **Abu Dawuud & Al-Hakim**

❷ On the authority of Ibn 'Abbaas that when the Messenger (pbuh) raised his head from rukuu' he said:

" حَمْدًا كَثِيرًا طَيِّبًا مُبَارَكًا فِيهِ – مِلءَ السَّمَاوَاتِ وَالأَرْضِ – وَ مِلءَ ما شِئْتَ مِنْ شَيءٍ بَعَد "

" أَهْلَ الثَّناءِ والمَجْدِ – لا مانِعَ لِما أَعْطَيْتَ ولا مُعْطِيَ لِما مَنَعْتَ – ولا يَنْفَعُ ذا الجَدِّ مِنْكَ الجَدُّ "

"Our Lord, for You all praise; an abundant beautiful blessed praise." **Bukhari**

"The heavens and the earth and all between them are abounding with Your praises, and all that You will abound with Your praises. O Possessor of all praise and majesty, the truest thing a slave has said (of You), and we are all Your slaves. O Allah, none can prevent what You have willed to bestow, and none can bestow what You have willed to prevent, and no wealth or majesty can benefit any one, as from You is all wealth and majesty." **Muslim**

❸ On the authority of Anas, he said: *"I will do my best to lead you in Salaat as the Messenger of Allah (pbuh) led us. When he raised his head from rukuu' he stood upright until people would think he forgot (the sujuud). And when he raised his head from sujuud, he sat still until people would think he forgot (the 2nd sujuud)."* **Agreed upon**

Common Errors

❶ Looking up to the sky/ceiling while raising the hands.

❷ Opening the palm up when saying supplications

❸ Not saying: "Rab-bana walaka al-hamdu."

A Golden Tip

❶ Allah loves to be praised. Praise Him by mentioning many forms of azkaar.

"Guard strictly as-Salaats, especially the middle Salaat, and stand before Allah with obedience." **2: 238**

Questions & Answers

Q1 What if one forgets to say Sami'a Allahu liman hamidah.

A If one is an imaam or an individual one has to make sujuud as-sahwi. But the ma'muum's Salaat is valid because the imaam is responsible for this.

Q2 Should one put the hands on the chest after rising from rukuu'?

A There are two strong opinions regarding this, the better of which is to place the hands back on the chest.

Q3 Should the maˆmuum say Sami'a Allahu liman hamidah?

A No, it is enough to say: "Rab-bana wa laka Al-hamdu" as the Messenger of Allah commanded people to do. **Muslim**

Q4 If the maˆmuum raises his head before or with the imaam, is his Salaat invalid?

A If done intentionally, it is invalid. But if done inadvertently, it is valid. The maˆmuum should always follow the imaam.

Imaam
The imaam says: (Sami'a Allahu liman hamidah) aloud; and "Rab-bana walaka al-hamdu" silently.

Maˆmuum
The maˆmuum says: "Rab-bana walaka al-humdu" silently.

Individual
Same as imaam but silently.

Males
No difference.

Females
No difference.

﴿ حَافِظُوا عَلَى الصَّلَوَاتِ وَالصَّلَاةِ الْوُسْطَىٰ وَقُومُوا لِلَّهِ قَانِتِينَ ﴾ البقرة ٢٣٨

Making 1st Sujuud

What

◆ Say: " اللَّهُ أَكْبَرُ "

"Allahu Akbar"
While in prostration,

◆ Say: " سُبْحانَ رَبِّيَ الأعْلى "

"Subhana rab-biya al-A'laa."
Meaning: Glory be to my
Lord, the Highest.

◆ Say:

"Allahu Akbar"

When

◆ After having said the supplication of standing after rising from rukuu'.

How

❶ Announce takbiir without raising the hands.

❷ Move down until you prostrate.

❸ Place the knees on the ground then the hands.

❹ Place the head on the ground.

❺ Keep the forehead and the nose on the ground.

❻ Place the hands on the ground parallel to shoulders.

❼ Keep the feet upright with the toes resting on the ground in the direction of the Qiblah.

Evidence

❶ The Messenger Muhammad (pbuh) used to keep his arms away from his body while performing sujuud. **Agreed upon**

❷ The Messenger (pbuh) said: *"I was commanded to prostrate on 7 bones: the forehead (and he pointed to the nose), the 2 hands, the 2 knees, and the toes."* **Agreed upon**

❸ You can also prostrate on a carpet, cloth, or a rug. On the authority of Anas, he said: *"We were praying with the Messenger (pbuh) in a very hot weather, and those of us who could not place their foreheads on the ground (because of the heat) extended their garments and prostrated on them."* **Agreed upon**

❹ Keep the arms parallel to the shoulders. On the authority of Abi Hamid that the Messenger (pbuh) used to place his nose and forehead on the ground, used to keep his arms away from his sides, and used to place his hands parallel to his shoulders. **Abu Dawuud & At-Termizi**

Common Errors

❶ Not letting the toes rest on the ground.
❷ Not letting the nose touch the ground.
❸ Rising from sujuud quickly.
❹ Placing the whole arm on the ground.

A Golden Tip

❶ Be diligent in your supplication. You can repeat it as many times as you wish because Allah loves those who ask Him with urgency.

"Celebrate the praises of your Lord and be of those who prostrate themselves in adoration." **15: 98**

السُّجُودُ الأوَّلُ

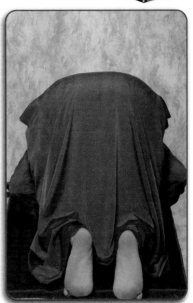

Questions & Answers

Q1 When should one do the 1st sujuud?

A After having announced takbiir.

Q2 Should one raise the hands when announcing takbiir?

A No.

Q3 How fast should one go down to prostration?

A Neither too fast to bother his neighbors on either side, nor too slow to show laziness.

Q4 How close to the body should the arms be?

A The Messenger of Allah (pbuh) used to keep his arms away from his body to the extent that his underarms would appear. **Agreed upon**

Q5 What is the correct position for the hands?

A Parallel to one's shoulders.
Abu Dawuud & At-Termizi

Imaam
The imaam announces takbiir for sujuud aloud.

Maˆmuum
The maˆmuum announces takbiir silently.

Individual
The individual announces takbiir silently.

All of them say: "Subhana rab-biya al-A'laa" silently.

Males
Males keep their arms away from their bodies.

Females
Females do not keep their arms away from their bodies if they fear that parts of their bodies might be uncovered.

﴿ فَسَبِّحْ بِحَمْدِ رَبِّكَ وَكُنْ مِّنَ السَّاجِدِينَ ﴾ الحجر ٩٨

Sitting Between the 2 Sujuuds

What

◆ During sitting, say:

رَبِّ اغْفِرْ لِي

"Rab-bi ighfir lee" (2 times)

Meaning: O Allah! Forgive me.

When

◆ After having announced takbiir for rising from the 1st sujuud.

How

❶ Sit down in a state of iftiraash.

❷ Let the top of the left foot touch the ground while the right foot remains upright.

❸ The toes face the Qiblah.

❹ Place the hands on the thighs close to the knees.

❺ Keep the fingers close to each other.

❻ Keep the eyes on the place of sujuud.

Evidence

❶ Abu Hurirrah said: the messenger of Allah advised the person who did not perform his Salaat properly to remain sitting until his limbs settle down during sitting. **Agreed Upon**

Common Errors

❶ Not resting in position long enough.

❷ Saying: "O Allah! Forgive me and forgive my parents" every time.

A Golden Tip

❶ Glorify Allah by following the Sun-nah of the Messenger of Allah (pbuh).

الجُلُوسُ بَيْنَ السَّجْدَتَيْنِ

Questions & Answers

1 Q Where should the hands be in between the 2 sajdahs?

A They should be on one's knees or thighs.

2 Q Where should one direct the sight?

A It should not wander beyond one's place of sujuud. This helps one concentrate.

3 Q Are there other supplications to be said in between the 2 sajdahs?

A Yes, but the above mentioned one is the most authentic.

4 Q How long should this sitting be?

A As along as it takes one's limbs to settle and finish the du'aaˆ, i.e. Just a few seconds.

5 Q What is the ruling on sitting on the heels or on the buttocks?

A It is prohibited.

Imaam
The imaam raises his voice in takbiir.
Maˆmuum
The maˆmuum does not.
Individual
The individual does not.

All of them say: "Rab_bi ighfir lee" silently.

Males
No difference.
Females
No difference.

﴿ رِجَالٌ لاَّ تُلْهِيهِمْ تِجَارَةٌ وَلا بَيْعٌ عَن ذِكْرِ اللَّهِ وَإِقَامِ الصَّلاةِ ﴾ النور ٣٧

Making 2nd Sujuud

What

◆ Say: " اللَّهُ أَكْبَرُ "

Allahu Akbar
While in prostration,

◆ Say: " سُبْحانَ رَبِّيَ الأَعْلى "

"Subhana rab-biya al-A'laa."
Meaning: Glory be to my
Lord, the Highest.

When

◆ After having said the supplication of sitting after the 1st rukuu'.

How

While announcing takbiir,

❶ Announce takbiir without raising the hands.

❷ Place the hands on the ground parallel to shoulders.

❸ Place the head on the ground.

❹ Keep the forehead and the nose on the ground.

❺ Keep the feet upright with the toes resting on the ground in the direction of the Qiblah.

Evidence

❶ In his explanation to the person who did not perform his Salaat properly, the Messenger Muhammad (pbuh) said: *"Say Allahu Akbar then prostrate until your joints rest completely."* **Agreed Upon**

❷ The Messenger (pbuh) said: *"I was commanded to prostrate on 7 bones: the forehead (and he pointed to the nose), the 2 hands, the 2 knees, and the toes."* **Agreed Upon**

❸ Again, keep the arms parallel to the shoulders. On the authority of Abi Hamid that the Messenger (pbuh) used to place his nose and forehead on the ground, and used to keep his arms away from his sides, and used to place his hands parallel to his shoulders." **Abu Dawood & At-Termizi**

Common Errors

❶ Not letting the toes rest on the ground.
❷ Not letting the nose touch the ground.
❸ Rising from sujuud quickly.

A Golden Tip

❶ The Messenger Muhammad (peace be unto him) taught that Allah loves those who are persistent in their supplications. So, try to be one of them.

"But celebrate the praises of your Lord, and be of those who prostrate themselves in adoration." **15: 98**

السُّجُودُ الثَّانِي

  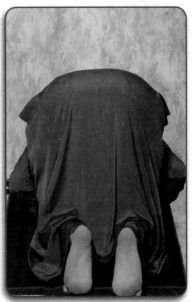

Questions & Answers

1 **Q** Can one say the supplications mentioned in the Qur'an verbatim while in sujuud?

A Yes, as long as the intention is not to recite the Qur'an itself.

2 **Q** Are there differences between the first and the second sujuud?

A No. But one can say different supplications.

3 **Q** Are there other types of tasbiih during sujuud?

A Yes. And these are mentioned at the end of the book under supplications.

4 **Q** How long can the sujuud be?

A It can be as long as the rukuu'.

5 **Q** Can one prolong the sujuud?

A Yes. It had been narrated that the Messenger Muhammad (pbuh) prolonged his sujuud during the night Salaat. However, when the imaam rises from sujuud, the ma'muum should follow him.

Imaam
The imaam announces takbiir for sujuud aloud.

Ma^muum
The ma^muum announces takbiir silently.

Individual
The individual announces takbiir silently.

All of them say: "Subhana rab-biya al-A'laa" silently.

Males
Keep their arms away from their bodies.

Females
Do not keep arms away from the bodies if they fear that parts of their bodies might be uncovered.

﴿ فَسَبِّحْ بِحَمْدِ رَبِّكَ وَكُن مِّنَ السَّاجِدِينَ ﴾ الحجر٩٨

What

◆ Say: " اللَّهُ أَكْبَرُ "

"Allahu Akbar"
  Meaning: Allah is Greater

◆ No opening supplication.

When

◆ After having finished the 2nd sujuud.

How

❶ Begin standing up until you become in the upright position.

❷ Announce takbiir while standing up.

❸ Keep looking at the place of sujuud.

Evidence

❶ "In 'Aaisha's (ra) description of the Salaat of the Messenger Muhammad (pbuh) she mentioned that he stood after the 2nd sujuud. **Muslim**

❷ When the Messenger of Allah (pbuh) stood for the 2nd rak'ah he started the rak'ah by reciting al-Fatihah directly with no period of silence (without saying the opening supplication). **Muslim**

❸ The Messenger Muhammad (pbuh) said: *"People should stop raising their eyes to the sky or their sights will be snatched."* **Muslim**

Common Errors

❶ Racing the imaam.
❷ Leaning against an object for no need.
❸ Losing the direction of the Qiblah.
❹ Raising the hands.

A Golden Tip

❶ Now you just have finished a whole rak'ah and started a totally new rak'ah, try your best to be more focused.

"O my Lord! Make me one who performs As-Salaat, and from my offspring, our Lord! And accept my invocation." **14: 40**

القِيامُ لِلرَّكْعَةِ الثَّانِيَةِ

Q1 Is resting during sitting before standing for the 2nd rak'ah a regular sun-nah?

A No, it is not. It is used only if needed.

Q2 Is there a specific zikr during the resting sitting?

A No. There is nothing specific. It is a very brief sitting.

Q3 If the imaam does not rest-sit, should the maˆmuum do it?

A It is always better to follow the imaam.

Q4 Is it a waajib to cover men's heads with any type of kufi?

A Wearing Kufi or something else on the head is not a waajib. Covering the head is not a condition for Salaat. However, in countries where it is customary to do so, it is recommended to be used. In some traditions, it is considered part of the ornament for men.

Q5 Is it permissible to read a short surah before a long one?

A Yes, but the sun-nah is to read the long one first.

Imaam
The imaam announces takbiir aloud.

Maˆmuum
The maˆmuum announces takbiir silently.

Individual
The individual announces takbiir silently.

Males
No difference

Females
No difference

﴿ رَبِّ اجْعَلْنِي مُقِيمَ الصَّلَاةِ وَمِن ذُرِّيَّتِي رَبَّنَا وَتَقَبَّلْ دُعَاءِ ﴾ إبراهيم ٤٠

Beginning 2nd Rakah
(Reciting the Qur'an)

What

◆ Recite al-Fatihah.

◆ Recite a surah or part of it.

When

◆ After having announced the takbiir.

◆ Place the hands on the chest.

How

While announcing takbiir,

❶ Say:"Bismillahi ar-Rahman ar-Rahim" silently.

❷ Recite al-Fatihah aloud.

❸ Recite a shorter surah than in the 1st rak'ah.

❹ Look at the place of sujuud.

❺ Place the hands on the chest; the right one on the left.

Evidence

❶ The Messenger of Allah (pbuh) used to recite in the 1st two rak'ahs the Fatihah and two surahs with the first surah being longer than the second. **Agreed upon**

❷ On the authority of Abu Sa'id al-Khudri (ra) that the Messenger of Allah (pbuh) used to recite in the 2nd rak'ah as much as half of the recitation in the 1st rak'ah.

Common Errors

❶ Saying the opening supplication in the 2nd rak'ah.

❷ Not reciting the basmalah.

❸ Not saying Aamen.

❹ Turning the face away from the place of sujuud.

❺ Not moving the lips while reciting Qur'an.

A Golden Tip

❶ Remember that "The best amongst you is the one who learns the Qur'an and teaches it to others." So spend more time learning the Qur'an.

"So, recite you of the Qur'an as much as may be easy for you." **73: 20**

قِرَاءَةُ الْقُرْآنِ

Questions & Answers

Q1 Are there specific surahs for every Ṣalaat?

A Not necessarily. However, on some days, the Messenger of Allah recited specific surahs such as al-A'laa and surah al-Ghashiyah on Fridays.

Q2 Should the Fatiḥah be recited in the 2nd rak'ah?

A Yes. al-Fatiḥah should be recited by the imaam, the ma^muum, and the individual in every rakah.

Q3 Can one recite more than one surah?

A Yes. The messenger (pbuh) read 3 surahs in one rak'ah during the night Ṣalaat.

Q4 Can one recite the same surah as in the 1st rak'ah?

A Yes. The Messenger Muḥammad (pbuh) recited surat al-Zalzalah twice in one Ṣalaat. **Abu Dawuud.**

Q5 What is the ruling on closing one's eyes during the Ṣalaat?

A It is disliked because it violates the sun-nah of the Messenger of Allah (pbuh) unless there is a reason such as strong light which may hurt the eyes, or the presence of some decoration that may cause distraction.

Imaam
The imaam recites al-Fatiḥah and Qur'an aloud (Fajr, Maghrib, and 'ishaa^)

Ma^muum
The ma^muum recites al-Fatiḥah and Qur'an silently.

Individual
The individual recites al-Fatiḥah and Qur'an silently.

Males
Males raise their voices while they say: "Aamen".

Females
Females do not.

﴿ فَاقْرَءُوا مَا تَيَسَّرَ مِنَ الْقُرْآنِ ﴾ المزمل ٢٠

Making Rukuu'

What

♦ Say: " اللَّهُ أَكْبَرُ "

"Allahu Akbar"
Meaning: Allah is Greater

♦ In bowing position, say:

" سُبْحانَ رَبِّيَ العَظِيمِ "

"Subhana rab-biya al-Aẓiim"
Meaning: Glory to my Lord, the Greatest.

When

♦ After having finished reciting the Qur'an announce takbiir while bowing down.

How

❶ Raise the hands as in the 1st takbiir.

❷ Bow down while announcing takbiir.

❸ Make both the head and the back parallel to the ground.

❹ Place the hands on the knees. Keep your fingers separated.

❺ Look at the place of sujuud.

Evidence

❶ The messenger of Allah (pbuh) said: *"If you bow place your palms on your knees; spread your fingers; and stay still until every body part rests back in place."* **Ibn Hib-ban**

❷ When the verse (Sabbih bismi rab-bika al-'Aẓiim) was revealed, the Messenger Muhammad said: *"Say it while doing rukuu'."* **Ahmad, Abu-Dawuud, & Ibn Majah**

Common Errors

❶ Not straightening the back.
❷ Not looking at the place of sujuud.
❸ Not placing the hands on the knees.
❹ Rushing the rukuuˆ.

A Golden Tip

❶ The sun-nah of the messenger of Allah (pbuh) is to make the time of rukuuˆ, sujuud, and standing almost equal.

"And perform As-Salaat, and give Zakaat, and bow down with obedience to Allah, along with ar-Raki'iin." **2: 43**

الرُّكُوعُ

Questions & Answers

Q1 How many times should one say "Subhana rab-biya al-Ażiim"?

A Once is required. However, one is recommended to say it more than once.

Q2 Are there du'aaˆs other than (Subhana rab-biya al-'Ażiim) during rukuu'?

A Yes. One such du'aaˆ is: " Sub-buuh, Qud-duus, Rab-bu-l- malaˆikati war-ruuh"

Q3 What if one says (Subhana Rab-biya al-A'laa instead of subhana rab-biya al-'Ażiim)?

A In case of the imaam or the individual, they should perform the sujuud of forgetfulness. The maˆmuum, however, should not because the imaam is responsible for this.

Q4 What if one forgets to do rukuu' and, instead, goes directly for sujuud?

A If one remembers before reaching the rukuu' of the following rakat, one should return immediately to make up the missed rukuu'. Then one should continue the rest of the Salaat. But If one remembers after having finished the rukuu' of the following rak'ah, one should not count the whole rak'ah in which the rukuu' was missed. In other words, one has to do another whole rak'ah instead. In both cases, one has to do sujuud of forgetfulness after the tasliim.

Imaam
The imaam raises his voice in takbiir.

Maˆmuum
The maˆmuum does not.

Individual
The individual does not.

Males
No difference.

Females
No difference.

﴿ وَأَقِيمُوا الصَّلَاةَ وَآتُوا الزَّكَاةَ وَارْكَعُوا مَعَ الرَّاكِعِينَ ﴾ البقرة ٤٣

A B C D E F G H I J K L M N O P Q R **S** T U V W X Y Z

Rising from Rukuu'

What

♦ While rising to the upright position, the imaam and the individual should say:

" سَمِعَ اللَّهُ لِمَنْ حَمِدَهُ "

"Sami'a Allahu liman hamidah."

♦ Then the imaam, ma'muums, and the individual should say:

" رَبَّنَا وَلَكَ الحَمْدُ "

"Rab-bana walaka al-hamd."

When

♦ After having finished the rukuu^.

How

❶ Raise the upper body back to its upright position.

❷ Raise the hands parallel to the shoulders or close to the lower ends of the ears.

❸ Keep your eyes on the place of sujuud.

Evidence

❶ The Messenger Muhammad (pbuh) advised the person who did not perform his Salaat well: *"Then say: "Sami'a Allahu liman hamidah. Then stand still."* **Abu Dawuud & Al-Hakim**

❷ On the authority of Ibn 'Abbaas that when the Messenger (pbuh) raised his head from rukuu' he said:

" حَمْدًا كَثِيرًا طَيِّبًا مُبَارَكًا فِيهِ – مِلءَ السَّمَاوَاتِ وَالأَرْضِ – وَ مِلءَ ما شِئْتَ مِنْ شَيْءٍ بَعَد

" أَهْلَ الثَّنَاءِ والمَجْدِ – لا مَانِعَ لِما أَعْطَيْتَ ولا مُعْطِيَ لِما مَنَعْتَ – ولا يَنْفَعُ ذا الجَدِّ مِنْكَ الجَدُّ "

"Our Lord, for You all praise; an abundant beautiful blessed praise." **Bukhari**

"The heavens and the earth and all between them are abounding with Your praises, and all that You will abound with Your praises. O Possessor of all praise and majesty, the truest thing a slave has said (of You), and we are all Your slaves. O Allah, none can prevent what You have willed to bestow, and none can bestow what You have willed to prevent, and no wealth or majesty can benefit any one, as from You is all wealth and majesty." **Muslim**

❸ On the authority of Anas, he said: *"I will do my best to lead you in Salaat as the Messenger of Allah (pbuh) led us. When he raised his head from rukuu' he stood upright until people would think he forgot (the sujuud). And when he raised his head from sujuud, he sat still until people would think he forgot (the 2nd sujuud)."* **Agreed upon**

Common Errors

❶ Looking up towards the sky or ceiling.

❷ Raising the hands (palms up) when saying supplications

❸ Touching the ears when raising the hands.

A Golden Tip

❶ Keeping your heart free of ill-feelings helps you focus on Salaat. It also makes you soft and gentle with Muslims. Showing them love and mercy is very important to keep the heart pure.

"Successful indeed are the believers. Those who offer their salaat with all solemnity and full submissiveness." **23:1-2**

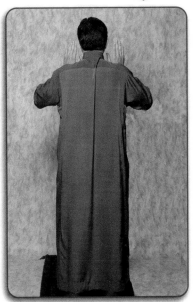

Questions & Answers

Q 1 Is it the sun-nah to touch the ears with the hands during rising from rukuu'?

A No. It is not the sun-nah to touch the ears in any situation in the Salaat.

Q 2 Some people do unnecessary movements such as playing with their beards, watches, mobiles. What is the ruling on that?

A Unnecessary movements are disliked. But too many unnecessary movements invalidate the Salaat.

Q 3 Can a woman pray while carrying her baby?

A Yes, if the baby is clean and not carrying him distracts her or others. The Messenger (peace be upon him) used to carry Umamah the daughter of Zainab.

Q 4 Can one say qunuut supplication after rising from rukuu' in the last rak'ah of the Salaat?

A No, except during calamities. The Messenger Muhammad (pbuh) did qunuut for a whole month in all the 5 Salaats (in the last rak'ah) when 70 memorizers of the Qur'an were killed.

Imaam
The imaam says: (Sami'a Allahu liman hamidah) aloud and "Rab-bana walaka al-hamd." silently.

Ma^muum
The ma^muum says: "Rab-bana walaka al-humd." silently.

Individual
The individual says: (Sami'a Allahu liman hamidah) and "Rab-bana walaka al-hamd." silently.

Males
No difference.

Females
No difference.

قَدْ أَفْلَحَ الْمُؤْمِنُونَ ۝ الَّذِينَ هُمْ فِي صَلَاتِهِمْ خَاشِعُونَ ۝ المؤمنون ٢.١

Making 1st Sujuud

What

◆ Say: " اللّهُ أَكْبَرُ "

"Allahu Akbar"
While in prostration,

◆ Say: " سُبْحانَ رَبِّيَ الأعْلى "

"Sub<u>h</u>ana rab-biya al-A'laa."
Meaning: Glory be to my
Lord, the Highest.

When

◆ After having said the supplication for standing after rising from rukuu'.

How

❶ Announce takbiir without raising the hands.

❷ Move down until you prostrate.

❸ Place the knees on the ground, then the hands.

❹ Place the head on the ground.

❺ Keep the forehead and the nose on the ground.

❻ Place the hands on the ground parallel to the head.

❼ Keep the feet upright with the toes resting on the ground in the direction of the Qiblah.

Evidence

❶ The Messenger of Allah (pbuh) used to keep his arms away from his body while performing sujuud.
Agreed upon

❷ The Messenger (pbuh) said: *"I was commanded to prostrate on 7 bones: the forehead (and he pointed to the nose), the 2 hands, the 2 knees, and the toes."* **Agreed upon**

❸ On the authority of Anas (ra), he said: *"We were praying with the Messenger (pbuh) in a very hot weather, and those of us who could not place their foreheads on the ground extended their garments and prostrated on them."* **Agreed upon**

❹ Keep your arms parallel to the shoulders. On the authority of Abi <u>H</u>amid that the Messenger (pbuh) used to place his nose and forehead on the ground, used to keep his arms away from his sides, and used to place his hands parallel to his shoulders. **Abu-Dawuud & At-Termi<u>z</u>i**

Common Errors

❶ Placing the whole arms on the ground.
❷ Spreading the fingers widely.
❸ Bothering others by opening arms widely.
❹ Bothering others by stretching the back.

A Golden Tip

❶ Prolong your sujuud and make your supplications comprehensive to include all Muslims.

"Celebrate the praises of your Lord and be of those who prostrate themselves in adoration." **15: 98**

السُّجُودُ الأوَّلُ

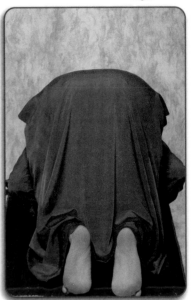

Questions & Answers

1 Q Is the sujuud of the 2nd rak'ah identical to the one of the 1st rak'ah?

A Yes, it is.

---

2 Q What should one do when catching up with the 1st sujuud of the 2nd rak'ah at Fajr Salaat?

A Do not wait. Announce takbiir (with the intention of takbirat al-Ihram) and prostrate directly. Continue until they finish the Salaat. Then do 2 rak'ahs by yourself because you did not catch the rukuu' of the 2nd rak'ah.

3 Q What is the ruling on having a barrier between the limbs of prostration (such as the head, the hands, the feet) and the ground?

A Yes, it is permissible to do sujuud on something between you and the ground whether this thing is connected to you such as a kufi, gloves, socks, etc.; or connected to the ground such as a rug or a carpet.

4 Q Which should touch the ground first, the knees or the hands?

A The knees first then the hands unless you are physically incapable. "You should not settle down like a camel."
Note: *Camels sit with the front legs (hands) first.*

Imaam
The imaam announces takbiir for sujuud aloud.
Maˆmuum
The maˆmuum announces takbiir silently.
Individual
The individual announces takbiir silently.
All of them say: "Subhana rab-biya al-A'laa" silently.

Males
Males keep their arms away from their bodies.

Females
Females do not do that if they fear that parts of their bodies might be uncovered.

﴿ فَسَبِّحْ بِحَمْدِ رَبِّكَ وَكُن مِّنَ السَّاجِدِينَ ﴾ الحجر ٩٨

Sitting After 1st Sujuud

What

◆ During sitting, say:

رَبِّ اغْفِرْ لِي

"Rab-bi ighfir lee" (2 times)

Meaning: O Allah!
Forgive me.

When

◆ After having announced takbiir for rising from the 1st sujuud.

How

❶ Sit down in a state of iftiraash.

❷ Let the top of the left foot touch the ground while the right foot remains upright.

❸ The toes face the Qiblah.

❹ Place the hands on the thighs close to the knees.

❺ Keep the fingers close to each other.

❻ Keep the eyes on the place of sujuud.

Evidence

❶ The companions who described the <u>S</u>alaat of the Messenger of Allah (pbuh) did not mention that he raised his hands in this position.

❷ On the authority of 'Aaisha (ra), the Messenger of Allah prohibited people from sitting on their heels like Satan. **Muslim**

Common Errors

❶ Not resting in this position long enough.

❷ Sitting on the two heels.

❸ Not looking at the place of sujuud.

A Golden Tip

❶ <u>S</u>alaat is so essential that it should not be missed even if one is extremely busy, sick, or even during engagement in a battle.

"And seek help in patience and As-<u>S</u>alaat and truly it is extremely heavy and hard except for al-Khashi'iin." **2: 45**

الجلُوسُ بيْنَ السّجْدتيْنِ

Questions & Answers

Q1 Is it permissible to raise/move one's index finger while sitting between the 2 sajdahs?

A Yes, it is because it is classified as (sitting) and the hadiith of Ibn 'Umar (ra) mentioned that.
Muslim

Q2 How long should this sitting be?

A As long as the sujuud.

Q3 Can one say a du'aaˆ other than the one mentioned by the Messenger (pbuh)?

A Yes, it is permissible. However, it is better to follow the sun-nah of the Messenger of Allah.

Q4 What if one forgets to say "Rab-bi ighfir lee"?

A No problem. No sujuud sahwi should be made for missing sun-nah.

Imaam
The imaam raises his voice in takbiir.
Maˆmuum
The maˆmuum does not.
Individual
The individual does not.

All of them say: "Rab-bi ighfir lee" silently.

Males
No difference.
Females
No difference.

﴿ وَاسْتَعِينُوا بِالصَّبْرِ وَالصَّلاةِ وَإِنَّهَا لَكَبِيرَةٌ إِلاَّ عَلَى الْخَاشِعِينَ ﴾ البقرة ٤٥

84

Making 2nd Sujuud

What

◆ Say: " اللَّهُ أَكْبَرُ "

"Allahu Akbar"
While in prostration.

◆ Say: " سُبْحَانَ رَبِّيَ الأَعْلَى "

"Subhana rab-biya al-A'laa."
Meaning: Glory be to my
Lord, the Highest

◆ Say:

"Allahu Akbar"
while rising from sujuud.

When

◆ After having said:
"Rab-bi ighfir lee."

How

❶ Announce takbiir without raising the hands.

❷ Place the hands on the ground parallel to the head.

❸ Place the head on the ground.

❹ Keep the forehead and the nose on the ground.

❺ Keep the feet upright with the toes resting on the ground in the direction of the Qiblah.

Evidence

❶ In his explanation to the person who did not perfect his Salaat, the Messenger of Allah (pbuh) said: *"Say Allahu Akbar, then prostrate until your joints rest completely."* **Agreed Upon**

❷ The Messenger of Allah (pbuh) said: *"I was commanded to prostrate on 7 bones: the forehead (and he pointed to the nose), the 2 hands, the 2 knees, and the toes."* **Agreed upon**

❸ On the authority of Abi Hamid that the Messenger (pbuh) used to place his nose and forehead on the ground, used to keep his arms away from his sides, and used to place his hands parallel to his shoulders. **Abu-Dawuud & At-Termizi**

Common Errors

❶ Placing the whole arms on the ground.
❷ Bothering others by opening the arms too widely.
❸ Sticking the arms to the body too tightly.
❹ Spreading the two feet widely.

A Golden Tip

❶ Remember that there is no guarantee that you might live long to do the next Salaat. Therefore, devote yourself entirely to the present Salaat as if it is the last one in your life.

"Celebrate the praises of your Lord and be of those who prostrate themselves in adoration." **15: 98**

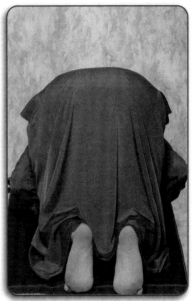

Questions & Answers

Q 1 If one enters the mosque and says a greeting (saying as-salamu 'alaikum, how is one in Salaat supposed to respond?

A One can respond by nodding or raising a hand slightly. **Ahmad**

Q 2 Should the 2nd sujuud be shorter than the first?

A No, they are equal.

Q 3 Are supplications during the 2nd sujuud different from the 1st one?

A "Subhana rab-biya al-A'ala" is the same. However, one can alternate between the authentic supplications said by the Messenger of Allah (pbuh) or can say own supplications.

Q 4 Does one raise the hands to do sujuud?

A No. On the authority of Ibn 'Umar (ra) He said: "The Messenger of Allah (pbuh) raised his hands in 4 positions; with takbirat al-ihram; at the rukuu'; upon rising from rukuu'; and upon rising from the 1st tashah-hud." **Muslim**

Imaam
The imaam announces takbiir for sujuud aloud.

Ma^muum
The ma^muum announces takbiir silently.

Individual
The individual announces takbiir silently.

All of them say: "Subhana rab-biya al-A'laa" silently.

Males
No difference.

Females
No difference.

﴿ فَسَبِّحْ بِحَمْدِ رَبِّكَ وَكُن مِّنَ السَّاجِدِينَ ﴾ الحجر ٩٨

Sitting for Tashah-hud

What

◆ Recite the tashah-hud.
(see page 94)

التَّحِيَّاتُ للَّهِ والصَّلَواتُ والطَّيِّبَاتُ.
السَّلَامُ عَلَيْكَ أَيُّها النَّبِيُّ وَرَحْمَةُ اللَّهِ وَبَرَكَاتُهُ
السَّلَامُ عَلَيْنَا
وَعَلَى عِبَادِ اللَّهِ الصَّالِحِينَ
أَشْهَدُ أَلَّا إِلَهَ إِلَّا اللَّهُ
وأَشْهَدُ أَنَّ مُحَمَّدًا عَبْدُهُ وَرَسُولُهُ.

When

◆ After having risen from the 2nd sujuud of the 2nd rak'ah.

How

❶ Sit down.
❷ Place the hands on the thighs. The left hand should be flat while the right one is closed, forming a circle with the middle finger and the thumb.
❸ Move the index finger of your right hand while saying supplications.
❹ Let the top of your left foot touch the ground while the right foot is upright. The toes face the Qiblah (Iftiraash)
❺ Look at your index finger.

Evidence

❶ "Aishah (ra) narrated that the Messenger of Allah used to sit in an Iftiraash form during the tashah-hud."
Muslim

❷ The position of the hands is explained by the <u>h</u>adiith of Ibn 'Umar who said: *"The messenger of Allah (pbuh), while sitting for tashah-hud, he used to open his left hand flat, close the right hand and point with his index finger."* **Muslim**

Common Errors

❶ Sitting on the heels.
❷ The right toes do not face the Qiblah.
❸ Bothering others by occupying a larger space when sitting in this position.

A Golden Tip

❶ Remember that an obligatory Salaat in congregation is 27 times better than praying alone.

"So, establish the Salaat as indeed Salaat is prescribed on believers at fixed times." 4:103

Questions & Answers

1 Q Are there differences in the sitting position for the two tashah-huds?

A In the first tashah-hud, one sits in the position of (iftiraash), whereas in the second one sits in the position of (tawar-ruk).

2 Q When can one move the index finger during the 1st tashah-hud?

A One can do so when saying a supplication.

3 Q Where should one look while reciting the 1st tashah-hud?

A At the index finger of the right hand.

4 Q Is there any supplication after the 1st tashah-hud?

A Yes. One is recommended to send greetings unto the Messenger of Allah (pbuh) from time to time by saying: (peace be unto him).

5 Q Can one prolong the 1st tashah-hud so as to include the Abrahamic Salaats?

A No. This is not the sunnah of the prophet. He used to say a brief 1st tashah-hud (1st part only).

Imaam
The imaam raises his voice in takbiir.
Maˆmuum
The maˆmuum does not.
Individual
The individual does not.

All of them: Recite the tashah-hud silently.

Males
No difference.
Females
No difference.

﴿ فَأَقِيمُوا الصَّلَاةَ إِنَّ الصَّلَاةَ كَانَتْ عَلَى الْمُؤْمِنِينَ كِتَابًا مَوْقُوتًا ﴾ النساء ١٠٣

Sitting for Last Tashah-hud

What

◆ Begin reciting the tashah-hud including the Abrahamic Salaats. *(see page 94)*

اللّٰهُمَّ صَلِّ عَلَى مُحَمَّدٍ
وَعَلَى آل مُحَمَّدٍ
كما صَلَّيْتَ عَلَى إبْراهِيمَ
وَعلى آل إبْراهِيمَ
وَبارِكْ عَلَى مُحَمَّدٍ
وَعَلَى آل مُحَمَّدٍ
كما بارَكْتَ عَلَى إبْراهِيمَ
وَعلى آل إبْراهِيمَ
فِي العالَمِينَ إنَّكَ حَمِيدٌ مَجِيدٌ

When

◆ After having risen from the 2nd sujuud of the last rak'ah.

How

❶ Announce takbiir without raising the hands.

❷ Sit in the position of (tawar-ruk) if doing a 3 or 4-rakah Salaat.

❸ The left foot should go under the right leg, the right foot should be upright; and the toes should face the Qiblah.

❹ The left hand is opened flat on the left thigh whereas the right hand is closed in the form of a circle and the index finger is moved up and down during the supplications.

❺ Keep your eyes on the index finger of the right hand.

Evidence

❶ Abdullah ibn al-Zubair said that when the Messenger of Allah would sit for the (last) tashah-hud, he would do so in the form of tawar-ruk. **Muslim**

Common Errors

❶ Not sitting in (tawar-ruk) position.

❷ Eyes are not focused on the index finger.

❸ Saying the word "say-yiidinah" before saying the Messenger of Allah (pbuh).

A Golden Tip

❶ Remember that moving your finger is heavier on Satan than a hammer's blow. Therefore, do not forget to move your finger during tashah-hud.

الجُلُوسُ لِلتَّشَهُّدِ الأخِيـر

Questions & Answers

Q1 If the Salaat has one tashah-hud only such as Friday Salaat or fajr Salaat, what is the position of the sitting for tashah-hud?

A It is iftiraash because tawar-ruk applies only to Salaats which have two tashahuds.

Q2 Where should one's sight be during the last tashahud?

A Look at your index finger.

Q3 What is the ruling on saying "say-yiidina" in the tashah-hud?

A No Muslim can deny that Muhammad is the master of mankind. This is part of the Islamic belief. However, since this phrase was not

mentioned by the Messenger (pbuh) himself, it is better to follow what he himself did.

Q4 Is there any supplication after the last tashahud?

A Yes. The following is the most authentic one: "O Allah! I take refuge with you from the torment of Hellfire; and from the torment of the grave; and from the tribulation of life and death; and from the evil of the false Messaiah."

" اللَّهُمَّ إِنِّي أَعُوذُ بِكَ مِنْ عَذابِ جَهَنَّمَ

وَمِنْ عَذابِ القَبْرِ

وَمِنْ فِتْنَةِ المَحْيا والمَمات

وَمِنْ شَرِّ فِتْنَةِ المَسِيحِ الدَّجَّالِ

Then one can say any other supplication related to worldly matters or the Afterlife.

Imaam
The imaam announces takbiir for sujuud aloud.
Maˆmuum
The maˆmuum does it silently.
Individual
The individual does it silently.

All of them: Recite the tashah-hud silently.

Males
No difference.
Females
No difference.

Making Tasliim

What

◆ Say:

" السَّلامُ عَلَيْكُمْ وَرَحْمَةُ اللَّهِ "

"As-salaamu 'alaikum wa rahmatu Allahi"
Meaning Peace be with you.

◆ Say the same thing while turning your face left.

When

◆ After having finished the tashah-hud.

How

❶ Turn your face to the right and say: "As-salaamu 'alaikum wa rahmatu Allahi"

❷ Then turn it to the left and say the same.

❸ Keep your hands flat on the thighs.

Evidence

❶ On the authority of 'Aisha (ra), she said that Muhammad (pbuh) made two tasliimahs. **Abu Dawuud**

❷ Sa'd ibn Abi Waq-qas (ra) narrated that he was able to view the Messenger's two cheeks from the back. **Muslim**

❸ "When the Salaat is ended, disperse in the land, and seek the Bounty of Allah." **62:10**

Common Errors

❶ Moving the right hand while turning right and the left hand while turning left.

❷ Not turning the face fully until the cheek can be viewed from the back.

❸ Doing tasliim with the imaam not after him.

❹ Prolonging the tasliim.

A Golden Tip

❶ Remember to make istighfaar as soon as you make tasliims. This is a cause to make Allah forgive the (errors) made during Salaat.

"Then when the Salaat is ended, you may disperse through the land, and seek the Bounty of Allah." **62:10**

Questions & Answers

 Q Are there other sayings for tasliim?

 A Yes. One can say:"as-salaamu 'alaikum warahmatu Allahi wa barakatuhu." when turning right.

Q Should one do tasliim after the imaam's each taslimah or when the imaam has finished the two tasliimahs together?

A Both are correct. However, it is recommended to do tasliim after the imaam has finished the 2 tasliimahs.

 Q What is the ruling on raising voices during the post-Salaat zikr after the 2nd tasliimah?

A Ibn 'Abbas (ra) narrated that raising voices with zikr was common at the time of the Messenger of Allah. **Agreed upon**

Q Is the Salaat considered complete if one does the 2nd tasliimah without saying zikr after the Salaat?

A Yes, it is. However, one misses the sun-nah of the Messenger of Allah (pbuh).

 Q What is the ruling on one who does one tasliimah only?

A No problem. His Salaat is complete.

Imaam
The imaam says salaams aloud.

Maˆmuum
The maˆmuum says salaams silently.

Individual
The individual says salaams silently.

Males
No difference.

Females
No difference.

Post-Salaat Checklist

Acts & Words	4	3	2	1
1. My heart contemplates the recitation in Salaat.				
2. I focus on the place of sujuud.				
3. I feel very peaceful after the Salaat.				
4. I recite different verses to keep myself mindful.				
5. I feel that I am addressing Allah in my Salaat.				
6. I alternate between different sunans.				
7. My rukuu' and sujuud are performed equally well.				
8. I offer my du'aaˆ consistently.				
9. I prolong my sujuud to offer more supplications.				
10. I perform all the authentic sunan of Salaat.				
11. I experience the spirit of unity with other Muslims.				
12. I feel contented with my performance in Salaat.				
13. I repent from my sins in my Salaat.				
14. My manners improve after my persisting on Salaat.				
15. I maintain my smile on my way to & from the masjid.				
16. I do my best to perform my Salaat similar to the Messenger's (pbuh).				
17. I sincerely ask Allah to guide me.				
18. I regularly make istigfaar and azkaar after the Salaat.				
19. I finish the sun-nah Salaat before I leave the masjid.				
20. I feel that my faith increases after my Salaat.				

4 = Very strongly   3 = Strongly   2 = Fair   1 = Weak

If you score in this range 70-80 you are excellent.
If you score in this range 50-69 you are fair.
If you score in this range 30-49 you need improvement.
If you score less than 30 you need a lot of work.

TOTAL SCORE

What is to be Spoken During <u>S</u>alaat

No.	Transliteration	Arabic	English Meaning
1.	Allaahu Akbar	اللهُ اكْبَرُ	Allah is Greater
2.	"Subhanaka-Allahum-ma wa bihamdika, watabaaraka-smuka, wata'aalaa jad-duka, walaa ilaaha ghayruka."	سُبْحَانَكَ اللّهُمَّ وَبِحَمْدِكَ، وَتَبَارَكَ اسْمُكَ وَتَعَالَى جَدُّكَ، وَلا إلَهَ غَيْرُكَ.	Glory and praise be to You O Allah. Blessed be Your Name, exalted be Your Majesty and Glory. There is no deity but You.
3.	A'uuzu bil-laahi mina-sh-shaytaani-r-rajim	اعُوذُ بِاللّهِ مِنَ الشَّيْطَانِ الرَّجِيم	I take refuge with Allah from the cursed devil.
4.	Bismil-laahi-r-Rahmaani-r-Rahiim	بِسْمِ اللّهِ الرَّحْمَنِ الرَّحِيم	In the name of Allah, the most Merciful, the Compassionate +surat Al-Fatihah. *(see page 99)*
5.	Allaahu Akbar	اللهُ اكْبَرُ	Allah is Greater
6.	Subhana Rabbiya-l-'Aziim	سُبْحَانَ رَبِّيَ العَظِيم	Glory be to Allah, the Greatest
7.	Sami'a-l-laahu liman hamidah	سَمِعَ اللّهُ لِمَنْ حَمِدَهُ	May Allah respond to those who praise Him
8.	Rab-banaa walaka-l-hamd Hamdan Kathiiran Tay-yiban Mubaarakan Fihi. Mil^a-s-samaawaati wa Mil^a-l-ard wa mil^a maa Baynahumaa Wa mil^a maa shi^ta min shay^in ba'd.	رَبَّنَا وَلَكَ الحَمْدُ، حَمْدًا كَثِيرًا طَيِّبًا مُبَارَكًا فيه، مِلءَ السَّمَاوَاتِ وَالأرْضِ، وَمِلءَ مَا بَيْنَهُما، وَ مِلءَ مَا شِئْتَ مِنْ شَيءٍ بَعْدُ ْ	Our Lord, All Praise is due to You, plentiful and blessed as to fill the heavens, the earth, all that is in between, and all that you please thereafter."
9.	Allaahu Akbar	اللهُ اكْبَرُ	Allah is Greater
10.	Subhaana Rab-biyya-l-A'laa	سُبْحَانَ رَبِّيَ الأعْلَى	Glory be to Allah, the Highest
11.	Allaahu Akbar	اللهُ اكْبَرُ	Allah is Greater
12.	Rab-bi-ghfir lii	رَبِّي اغْفِرْ لِي	Oh Allah! Forgive me.
13.	Allaahu Akbar	اللهُ اكْبَرُ	Allah is Greater
14.	Subhaana Rab-biyya-l-A'laa	سُبْحَانَ رَبِّيَ الأعْلَى	Glory be to Allah, the Highest
15.	Allaahu Akbar	اللهُ اكْبَرُ	Allah is Greater
16.	At-tahiyyaatu Lil-laahi was-salawaatu wat-tay-yibaatu Assalaamu alayka ayyuha-nnabiyyu wa rahmatullaahi wa barakaatuhu. Assalaamu 'alaynaa wa'alaa 'ibaadil-lahi-s-saalihin. Ash-hadu al-laa ilaaha il-la-Allahu, Wa ash-hadu an-na Muhammadan 'abudhu warasuuluhu. Allahum-ma salli 'alaa Muhammadin wa 'alaa aali Muhammad. Kamaa sal-layta 'alaa Ibraahima wa 'laa aali Ibrhaaim. Wa baarik alaa Muhammadin wa 'alaa aali Muhammad. Kamaa baarakta 'alaa Ibraahim wa 'alaa aali Ibraahim. innaka hamidun majiid.	التَّحِيَّاتُ لِلّهِ والصَّلواتُ والطَّيِّبَاتُ. السَّلَامُ عَلَيْكَ ايُّها النَّبِيُّ وَرَحْمَةُ اللّهِ وَبَرَكاتُهُ السَّلامُ عَلَيْنا وَعَلَى عِبادِ اللّهِ الصَّالِحِينَ اشْهَدُ الأ إلَهَ إلأ اللّهُ واشْهَدُ انَّ مُحَمَّدًا عَبْدُهُ وَرَسُولُهُ. اللّهُمَّ صَلِّ عَلَى مُحَمَّدٍ وَعَلَى آلِ مُحَمَّدٍ كما صَلَّيْتَ عَلَى إبْراهِيمَ وَعلى آلِ إبْراهِيمَ وَبَارِكْ عَلَى مُحَمَّدٍ وعَلى آلِ مُحَمَّدٍ كما بارَكْتَ عَلَى إبْراهِيمَ وَعلى آلِ إبْراهِيمَ فِي العالَمِينَ إنَّكَ حَمِيدٌ مَجِيدٌ	All greetings, Salaats, and blessings belong to Allah. Peace, mercy and the blessing of Allah be on you, O Prophet. May peace be upon us and on the righteous slaves of Allah. I testify that there is no deity worthy of worship but Allah. I testify that Muhammad is His slave and messenger. O Allah, bless Muhammad and his family as You blessed Ibrahim and his family. You are the Most-Praised, the Most-Glorious. O Allah, bestow Your grace on Muhammad and his family as You bestowed it on Ibrahim and his family. You are the Most-Praised, the Most – Glorious.
17.	As-salamu 'alaykum wa rahmatul-l-laahi	السَّلامُ عَلَيْكُمْ وَرَحْمَةُ اللّهِ	Peace and blessings be unto you.
18.	As-salaamu 'alayikum wa rahmatul- l-laahi	السَّلامُ عَلَيْكُمْ وَرَحْمَةُ اللّهِ	Peace and blessings be unto you.

A Comparison between Imaam & Maˆmuum

Differences between the Imaam and the Maˆmumm are based on their roles in the Salaats and should be meticulously observed. ('Ishaaˆ Salaat)

Imaam	Step	Maˆmuum
The 1st Rak'ah		
In the heart No Articulation	Intention	In the heart No Articulation
Announcing: "Allaahu akbar" Aloud	Takbiratu-l ihraam	Announcing: "Allahu Akbar" Silently
Reciting the Fatihah Aloud	Reciting The Fatihah	Listen to Imaam's recitation then recite the Fatihah Silently
Saying: "Aameen" Aloud	Saying: "Aameen"	Saying: "Aameen" Aloud
Reciting the Qu'ran Aloud	Reciting Qur'an	Listening to the Qu'ran
Announcing: "Allaahu akbar" Aloud	Rukuu' Takbiir	Announcing: "Allaahu Akbar" Silently
Saying: "Subhana rab-biya-l-'Ażiim" Silently	Bowing	Saying: "Subhana rab-biya-l-'Ażiim" Silently
Saying: "Sami'a-llaahu liman hamidah" Aloud Saying: "Rab-bana walaka-l-hamd" Silently	Rising from Rukuu'	Saying: "Rab-bana walaka-l-hamd" Silently
Offering other supplications Silently	Brief standing	Offering other supplications Silently
Announcing: "Allaahu akbar" Aloud	Takbiir for the 1st sujuud	Announcing: "Allaahu akbar" Silently
Saying: "Subhana rab-biya-l-A'laa" Silently	1st sujuud	Saying: "Subhana rab-biya- l-A'laa" Silently
Announcing: "Allaahu akbar" Aloud	Rising from the 1st sujuud	Saying: "Allaahu akbar" Silently
Saying: "Rab-bi ighfir lee" Silently	Sitting between the 2 sujuuds	Saying: "Rab-bi ighfir lee" Silently
Announcing: "Allaahu akbar" Aloud	Takbiir for the 2nd sujuud	Saying: "Allaahu akbar" Silently
Saying: "Subhana rab-biya-l-A'laa" Silently	The 2nd sujuud	Saying: "Subhana rab-biya-l-A'laa Silently
Announcing: "Allaahu akbar" Aloud	Rising from the 2nd sujuud	Saying: "Allaahu akbar" Silently

A Comparison between Imaam & Maˆmuum

Differences between the Imaam and the Maˆmumm are based on their roles in the Ṣalaats and should be meticulously observed ('Ishaaˆ Ṣalaat).

Imaam	Step	Maˆmuum
The 2nd Rak'ah		
The Second Rak'ah is exactly the same except that, at the end, you sit down for the 1st tashah-hud instead of standing to begin another rak'at.		
Reciting At-tashah-hud Silently	Reciting At-tashah-hud	Reciting At-tashah-hud Silently
Saying Allaahu Akbar Aloud	Standing for the 3rd rak'ah	Saying Allaahu Akbar Silently
The 3rd Rak'ah		
In the 3rd rak'ah, the imaam reads the Fatiḥah silently as well as the maˆmuum. There is no recitation of the Qur'an. Everything else is the same.		
Saying Allaahu Akbar Aloud	Standing for 3rd rak'ah	Saying Allaahu Akbar Silently
The 4th Rak'ah		
The 4th rak'at is exactly like the 3rd one. The only difference is that there is no standing after the 2nd sujuud. Instead, both the imaam and maˆmuum will sit for the 2nd tashah-hud.		
Saying Allaahu Akbar Aloud	Sitting for the 2nd tashah-hud	Saying Allaahu Akbar Silently
Reciting At-tashah-hud Silently	Reciting the whole tashah-hud including the Abrahamic Ṣalaats	Reciting At-tashah-hud Silently
Saying Assalaamu alaykum waraḥmatu-l-laah Aloud	Performing the 1st tasliimah	Saying Assalaamu alaykum waraḥmatu-l-laah Silently
Saying Assalaamu alaykum waraḥmatu-l-laah Aloud	Performing the 2nd tasliimah	Saying Assalaamu alaykum waraḥmatu-l-laah Silently

Aloud means audible to others.
Silently means articulation to oneself.

A Comparison between Males & Females

This is for when both men and women are maˆmuum. When performing Salaat individually, their Salaat is exactly the same.

Males	Step	Females
The 1st Rak'ah		
In the heart No Articulation	Intention	In the heart No Articulation
Saying: "Allaahu Akbar" Silently	Takbiratu-l ihraam	Saying: "Allahu Akbar" Silently
Listen to Imaam's recitation then recite the Fatihah Silently	Reciting The Fatihah	Listen to Imaam's recitation then recite the Fatihah Silently
Saying: "Aameen" Silently	Saying: "Aameen"	Saying: "Aameen" Silently
Listening	Reciting Qur'an	Listening
Saying: "Allaahu Akbar" Silently	Rukuu' Takbiir	Saying: "Allaahu Akbar" Silently
Saying: "Subhana rab-biya-l-'Ażiim" Silently	Bowing	Saying: "Subhana rab-biya-l-'Ażiim" Silently
Saying: "Rab-bana walaka-l-hamd" Silently	Rising from Rukuu'	Saying: "Rab-bana walaka-l-hamd" Silently
Offering other supplications Silently	Brief standing	Offering other supplications Silently
Saying: "Allaahu Akbar" Silently	Takbiir for the 1st sujuud	Saying: "Allaahu Akbar" Silently
Saying: "Subhana rab-biya-l-A'laa" Silently	1st sujuud	Saying: "Subhana rab-biya- l-A'laa" Silently
Saying: "Allaahu Akbar" Silently	Rising from the 1st sujuud	Saying: "Allaahu Akbar" Silently
Saying: "Rab-bi ighfir lii" Silently	Sitting between The 2 sujuuds	Saying: "Rab-bi ighfir lii" Silently
Saying: "Allaahu Akbar" Silently	Takbiir for the 2nd sujuud	Saying: "Allaahu Akbar" Silently
Saying: "Subana rab-biya-l-A'laa" Silently	The 2nd sujuud	Saying: "Subhana rab-biya-l-A'laa" Silently
Saying: "Allaahu Akbar" Silently	Rising from the 2nd sujuud	Saying: "Allaahu Akbar" Silently

A Comparison between Males & Females

This is for when both men and women are maˆmuum. When performing <u>S</u>alaat individually, their <u>S</u>alaat is exactly the same.

Males	Step	Females
The 2nd Rak'ah		
The Second Rak'ah is exactly the same except that, at the end, you sit down for the 1st tashah-hud instead of standing to begin another rak'at.		
Reciting At-tashah-hud Silently	Reciting At-tashah-hud	Reciting At-tashah-hud Silently
Saying Allaahu Akbar Silently	Standing for the 3rd rak'ah	Saying Allaahu Akbar Silently
The 3rd Rak'ah		
In the 3rd rak'ah, the imaam reads the Fatihah silently as well as the maˆmuum. There is no recitation of the Qur'an. Everything else is the same.		
Saying Allaahu Akbar Silently	Standing for 3rd rak'ah	Saying Allaahu Akbar Silently
The 4th Rak'ah		
The 4th rak'at is exactly like the 3rd one. The only difference is that there is no standing after the 2nd sujuud. Instead, both the imaam and maˆmuum will sit for the 2nd tashah-hud.		
Saying Allaahu Akbar Silently	Sitting for the 2nd tashah-hud	Saying Allaahu Akbar Silently
Reciting the whole tashah-hud Silently	Reciting the whole tashah-hud including the Abrahamic <u>S</u>alaats	Reciting the whole tashah-hud Silently
Saying Assalaamu alaykum wara<u>h</u>matu-l-laah Silently	Performing the 1st tasliimah	Saying Assalaamu alaykum warahmatu-l-laah Silently
Saying Assalaamu alaykum wara<u>h</u>matu-l-laah Silently	Performing the 2nd tasliimah	Saying Assalaamu alaykum warahmatu-l-laah Silently

The only difference is in saying Aameen. Men say it aloud whereas women say it silently.

Al-Fatihah   The Opening

No.	Transliteration	Arabic	English Meaning
1.	BissmiLahi ir-Rahmani ir-Rahiim	بِسۡمِ ٱللّٰهِ ٱلرَّحۡمٰنِ ٱلرَّحِيمِ ①	In the name of Allah, the Most Merciful, the Most Compassionate.
2.	Al-Hamdu Lilahi Rabbi al'aalamiin	ٱلۡحَمۡدُ لِلّٰهِ رَبِّ ٱلۡعٰلَمِينَ ②	All Praise belongs to Allah, The Lord of the worlds.
3.	Ar-Rahmani ir-Rahiim	ٱلرَّحۡمٰنِ ٱلرَّحِيمِ ③	The Most Merciful, the Most Compassionate.
4.	Maliki Yawmi ed-Diin	مٰلِكِ يَوۡمِ ٱلدِّينِ ④	The Owner of the Day of Repayment.
5.	Iyyaka na'budu Wa Iy-yaka nasta'een	إِيَّاكَ نَعۡبُدُ وَإِيَّاكَ نَسۡتَعِينُ ⑤	You alone we worship, and You alone we call for help.
6.	Ihdina as-Sirata al-Mustaqiim	ٱهۡدِنَا ٱلصِّرٰطَ ٱلۡمُسۡتَقِيمَ ⑥	Guide us to the Straight Way.
7.	Siratal al-lazina an'amta 'alaihim	صِرٰطَ ٱلَّذِينَ أَنۡعَمۡتَ عَلَيۡهِمۡ	The Way of those on whom You bestowed Your Grace.
	Ghairil el-maghdubi 'Alaihim	غَيۡرِ ٱلۡمَغۡضُوبِ عَلَيۡهِمۡ	Not the way of those who earned Your Anger.
	Wala Ad-daaliin	وَلَا ٱلضَّآلِّينَ ⑦	Nor of those who have gone astray.

Supplications of Salaat أَدْعِيَةُ الصَّلَاةِ

- Here are some of the most authentic supplications of Salaat.
- These supplications are listed in order, from the most common to the least common.
- If there is more than one authentic du'aâ, it is better to alternate between them.
  It is better not to stick to a single one.

Opening Supplications أَدْعِيَةُ الاسْتِفْتَاحِ

No.	Transliteration	Arabic	English Meaning
1.	"Allahum-ma baa'id baynii wa bayna khatayaaya kamaa baa'adta bayna-l-mashriqi wa-l-maghrib. Allaahumma naq-qinii min khatayaaya kamaa yunaqqa-th-thawbu-l-abyadu mina-d-danas. Allahum-ma-ghsilnii min khatayaaya bi-th-thalji wa-l-maaˆi wa-l-barad." **Bukhari & Muslim**	"اللَّهُمَّ بَاعِدْ بَيْنِي وَبَيْنَ خَطَايَايَ كَما بَاعَدْتَ بَيْنَ الْمَشْرِقِ وَالْمَغْرِبِ. اللَّهُمَّ نَقِّنِي مِنْ خَطَايَايَ كَمَا يُنَقَّى الثَّوْبُ الأَبْيَضُ مِنَ الدَّنَسِ. اللَّهُمَّ اغْسِلْنِي مِنْ خَطَايَايَ بِالثَّلْجِ وَالمَاءِ وَالبَرَدِ" (البُخَارِي وَمُسْلِم)	"O Allah! Distance me from my sins as You distanced The East from the West. O Allah! purify me from my sins as a white garment is purified from filth. O Allah! Cleanse me of my sins with snow, water and ice." **Agreed upon**
2.	"Subhaanaka-l-laahumma wa bihamdika Wa tabaaraka-smuka. Wa ta'aalaa jad-duka. Wa laa ilaaha ghayruka." **Abu Dawood**	"سُبْحَانَكَ اللَّهُمَّ وَبِحَمْدِكَ، وَتَبَارَكَ اسْمُكَ وَتَعَالَى جَدُّكَ، وَلَا إِلَهَ غَيْرُكَ" (أَبُو دَاود)	"Glory and praise be to you O Allah! Blessed be your name, and lofty is Your position, and there is no deity but You." **Abu Dawuud**
3.	"Waj-jahtu Wajhi li-l-lazi fatara-s-samaawaati wa-l-ard haniifan wa maa ana mina-l-mushrikiin. Inna Salaati wa nusuki wa mahyaaya wa mamaati lil-laahi rab-bil 'aalamiin-laa shariika lahu wa bizalika umirtu wa ana mina-l-muslimiin." **Muslim**	"وَجَّهْتُ وَجْهِيَ لِلَّذِي فَطَرَ السَّمَاوَاتِ وَالأَرْضَ حَنِيفًا، وَمَا أَنَا مِنَ المُشْرِكِينَ، إِنَّ صَلَاتِي وَنُسُكِي وَمَحْيَايَ وَمَمَاتِي لِلَّهِ رَبِّ العَالَمِينَ، لَا شَرِيكَ لَهُ وَبِذَلِكَ أُمِرْتُ، و أَنَا مِنَ المُسْلِمِينَ" (مُسْلِم)	"I turned my face sincerely towards He who brought forth the Heavens and the Earth, and I am not of those who associate (others with Allah). Indeed my salaat, my sacrifice, my life, and my death are for Allah, the Lord of the Worlds. There are no partners with Him. With this I am commanded and I am one of the Muslims." **Muslim**

Supplications of Rukuu' أَدْعِيَةُ الرُّكُوعِ

No.	Transliteration	Arabic	English Meaning
1.	"Subhana rabiy-ya-l-'aziim." **Abu Dawood**	"سُبْحَانَ رَبِّيَ العَظِيمِ" (أَبُو دَاود)	"O Allah! How perfect You are, the Supreme." **Abu Dawuud**
2.	"Sub-buuh Qud-duus Rab-bu-l-malaaˆikati war-ruuh." **Muslim**	"سُبُّوحٌ قُدُّوسٌ، رَبُّ الَمَلائِكَةِ وَالرُّوحِ" (مُسْلِم)	"Perfect and Holy He is, the Lord of angels and Ruuh. (Gibreel)" **Muslim**
3.	"Allahum-ma laka raka'atu wa bika aamantu walak aslamtu- khasha'a laka sam'ii wa basarii wa mukh-khii wa 'azmii wa 'asabi wa mastaqal-la bihi qadamii." **Muslim**	"اللَّهُمَّ لَكَ رَكَعْتُ، وَبِكَ آمَنْتُ، وَلَكَ أَسْلَمْتُ، خَشَعَ لَكَ سَمْعِي وَبَصَرِي، وَمُخِّي وَعَظْمِي، وما اسْتَقَلَّ بِهِ قَدَمِي" (مُسْلِم)	"O Allah! Unto You I have bowed, and in You I have believed, and to You I have submitted. My hearing, sight, mind, bones, tendons and what my feet carry are humbled before you." **Muslim**

Supplications of Rising from Rukuu'

أَدْعِيَةُ الرَّفْعِ مِنَ الرُّكُوعِ

No.	Transliteration	Arabic	English Meaning
1.	"Sami'a-l-laahu liman Hamidah." **Bukhari**	<div dir="rtl">"سَمِعَ اللَّهُ لِمَنْ حَمِدَهُ" (البُخَاري)</div>	"May Allah answer he who praises Him." **Bukhari**
2.	"Rab-banaa wa laka-l-hamd. Hamdan kathiiran tay-yiban mubaarakan fiihi." **Bukhari**	<div dir="rtl">"رَبَّنَا وَلَكَ الحَمْدُ، حَمْدًا كَثِيرًا طَيِّبًا مُبَارَكًا فِيهِ ،</div>	"Our Lord, for You all praise; an abundant beautiful blessed praise." **Bukhari**
3.	"Mil-ˆas-samaawaati wa milˆa-l-ard wamilˆa maa baynahumaa. Wa milˆa maa shiˆta min shay^in ba'd ahla-th-thanaaˆi wal-majd ahaqqa maa qaalahu-l-'abd wakul-lunaa laka'abd laa maani'inI limaa a'atayta- walaa mu'tiya limaa mana'ta- walaa yanfa'u za-l- jaddi minka-l-jadd." **Muslim**	<div dir="rtl">مِلْءَ السَّمَاوَاتِ وَالأَرْضِ، وَمِلْءَ ما بَيْنَهُما، وَ مِلْءَ ما شِئْتَ مِنْ شَيْءٍ بَعْدُ ، أَهْلَ الثَّنَاءِ والمَجْدِ ، أَحَقُّ ما قَالَهُ العَبْدُ، وَكُلُّنا لَكَ عَبْدٌ، لا مانِعَ لِما أَعْطَيْتَ، ولا مُعْطِيَ لِما مَنَعْتَ، وَلا يَنْفَعُ ذا الجَدِّ مِنْكَ الجَدُّ" (مُسْلِم)</div>	"The heavens and the earth and all between them are abounding with Your praises, and all that You will abound with Your praises. O Possessor of all praise and majesty, the truest thing a slave has said (of You), and we are all Your slaves. O Allah, none can prevent what You have willed to bestow, and none can bestow what You have willed to prevent, and no wealth or majesty can benefit any one, as from You is all wealth and majesty." **Muslim**

Supplications of Sujuud

أَدْعِيَةُ السُّجُودِ

No.	Transliteration	Arabic	English Meaning
1.	"Subhaana rab-biya-l-A'laa." **Al-Termizi**	<div dir="rtl">"سُبْحَانَ رَبِّيَ الأَعْلَى" (الترمذي)</div>	"How perfect You are, the Most High." **Al-Termizi**
2.	"Allahum-ma laka sajadtu- wabika aamantu- walaka aslamtu- sajada wajhii lil-lazii kha-laqahu wasawwarahu wa shaq-qa sam'ahu wabasarahu- tabaaraka-llaahu ahsanu-l-khaaliqiin." **Muslim**	<div dir="rtl">"اللَّهُمَّ لَكَ سَجَدْتُ ، وَبِكَ آمَنْتُ ، وَلَكَ أَسْلَمْتُ، سَجَدَ وَجْهِي لِلَّذِي خَلَقَهُ وَصَوَّرَهُ، وَشَقَّ سَمْعَهُ وَبَصَرَهُ، تَبَارَكَ اللَّهُ أَحْسَنُ الخَالِقِينَ" (مُسْلِم)</div>	"O Allah! Unto You I have prostrated and in You I have believed, and unto You I have submitted. My face has prostrated before He Who created it and fashioned it, and brought forth its faculties of hearing and seeing. Blessed is Allah, the best of creators." **Muslim**
3.	"Allahum-ma-ghfir lii zanbi kullahu, diq-qahu wa jul-lahu , wa aw-waluhu wa aakhirahu , wa alaaniyatahu wasir-rahu." **Muslim**	<div dir="rtl">"اللَّهُمَّ اغْفِرْ لِي ذَنْبِي كُلَّهُ، دِقَّهُ وَجِلَّهُ، وَأَوَّلَهُ وَآخِرَهُ، وَعَلانِيَتَهُ وَسِرَّهُ" (مُسْلِم)</div>	"O Allah! Forgive me all of my sins, the small and the great of them, the first and the last of them, and the seen and the hidden of them." **Muslim**
4.	"Allahum-ma a'uuzu biridaaka min sakhatika, wa bimu'aafaatika min'uuqubatika, wa a'uuzu bika minka laa uhsii thanaaˆ an'alayka anta kamaa athnayta 'alaa nafsika." **Muslim**	<div dir="rtl">"اللَّهُمَّ أَعُوذُ بِرِضَاكَ مِنْ سَخَطِكَ، وَبِمُعَافَاتِكَ مِنْ عُقُوبَتِكَ ،وَأَعُوذُ بِكَ مِنْكَ لا أُحْصِي ثَنَاءً عَلَيْكَ، أَنْتَ كَمَا أَثْنَيْتَ عَلَى نَفْسِكَ" (مُسْلِم)</div>	"O Allah! I take refuge within Your pleasure from Your displeasure and within Your pardon from Your punishment. And I take refuge in You from You. I cannot enumerate Your praise. You are as You have praised Yourself." **Muslim**
5.	"Subhaanaka-llahum-ma wa bihamdika laa ilaaha illa anta Allaahumma-ghfir lee." **Muslim**	<div dir="rtl">"سُبْحَانَكَ اللَّهُمَّ وَبِحَمْدِكَ، لا إِلَهَ إِلَّا أَنْتَ، اللَّهُمَّ اغْفِرْ لِي" (مُسْلِم)</div>	"How perfect You are O Allah, our Lord, and I praise You. O Allah, for give me." **Muslim**
6.	"Sub-buuh Qud-duus rab-bul malaaˆikati war-ruuh." **Muslim**	<div dir="rtl">"سُبُّوحٌ قُدُّوسٌ رَبُّ الْمَلَائِكَةِ وَالرُّوحُ" (مُسْلِم)</div>	"Perfect and Holy (He is), Lord of the angels and the Ruuh (Gabril)." **Muslim**

Supplications between 2 Sujuuds

أَدْعِيَةُ مَا بَيْنَ السَّجْدَتَيْنِ

No.	Transliteration	Arabic	English Meaning
1.	"Rabbi-ghfir lii- Rab-bi-ghfir lii." **Abu-Dawood**	"رَبِّ اغْفِرْ لِي، رَبِّ اغْفِرْ لِي" (أَبُو داود)	"O My Lord! Forgive me. O My Lord! Forgive me." **Abu Dawuud**
2.	"Allahum-ma-ghfir lii war-hamnii waj-burnii wah-dinii war-zuqnii war-fa'anii." **Abu-Dawood**	"اللَّهُمَّ اغْفِرْ لِي وَارْحَمْنِي وَاجْبُرْنِي وَاهْدِنِي وَارْزُقْنِي وَارْفَعْنِي" (أَبُو داود)	"O Allah! Forgive me, and have mercy on me, enrich me, give me health, grant me sustenance, and give me rank." **Abu Dawuud**

Supplications after the 2nd tashah-hud

أَدْعِيَةُ مَا بَعْدَ التَّشَهُّدِ الأَخِيرِ

No.	Transliteration	Arabic	English Meaning
1.	"Allahum-ma innai a'uuzu bika min'azaabi jahannam wa min'azaabil qabri wa min fitnatil mahyaa wa-l-mamaati- wa min sharri fitnatil masiihi-ddajjaal." **Bukhari & Muslim**	"اللَّهُمَّ إِنِّي أَعُوذُ بِكَ مِنْ عَذَابِ جَهَنَّمَ، وَمِنْ عَذَابِ الْقَبْرِ، وَمِنْ فِتْنَةِ الْمَحْيَا والمَمَاتِ، وَمِنْ فِتْنَةِ الْمَسِيحِ الدَّجَّالِ" (البخاري ومسلم)	"O Allah! I take refuge in You from the punishment of the grave, from the torment of the fire, from the tribulations of life and death, and from the evil affliction of the Dajjal (false Messiah)." **Bukhari & Muslim**
2.	"Allahum-ma innii zalamtu nafsii zulman kathiiran wa laa yaghfiru-z-znuuba illaa anta fa-ghfir lii maghfiratan min 'indika war-hamnii innaka anta-l-ghafuuru-r-rahiim." **Bukhari**	"اللَّهُمَّ إِنِّي ظَلَمْتُ نَفْسِي ظُلْمًا كَثِيرًا، وَلا يَغْفِرُ الذُّنُوبَ إِلاَّ أَنْتَ، فَاغْفِرْ لِي مَغْفِرَةً مِنْ عِنْدِكَ، وَارْحَمْنِي، إِنَّكَ أَنْتَ الْغَفُورُ الرَّحِيمُ" (البخاري)	"O Allah! I have indeed wronged my soul excessively and none can forgive my sins but You. So grant me forgiveness from Yourself, and have mercy on me, You are the Most-Forgiving, the Most-Merciful." **Bukhari**
3.	"Allahum-ma-ghfir lii maa qaddamtu wamaa akh-khartu wa maa asrartu wa maa a'lantu wa maa anta a'lamu bihi minnii anta-l- muqaddimu wa anta-l-mu^akh-khiru laa ilaah illa anta." **Muslim**	"اللَّهُمَّ اغْفِرْ لِي مَا قَدَّمْتُ وَمَا أَخَّرْتُ، وَما أَسْرَرْتُ وَمَا أَعْلَنْتُ، وما أَنْتَ أَعْلَمُ بِهِ مِنِّي، أَنْتَ الْمُقَدِّمُ وَأَنْتَ الْمُؤَخِّرُ، لا إِلَهَ إِلاَّ أَنْتَ" (مسلم)	"O Allah! Forgive me for those sins which have come to pass as well as those which will come, and those I have committed in secret, and those I have committed in public, and where I have exceeded all bounds as well as those things about which You are more knowledgeable. You are the Muqad-dim and the Mu^akh-khir. None but You is worth of worship." **Muslim**

Supplications Qunuut

دُعَاءُ الْقُنُوتِ

No.	Transliteration	Arabic	English Meaning
1.	"Allahum-ma-hdinii fiiman hadayta wa 'aafinii fiiman 'aafayta wa tawal-lanii ifiman tawal-layta wa baarik lii fiimaa a'tayta wa qinii shar-ra maa qadayta fa^innaka taqdii walaa yuqdaa 'alayka wa innahu laa yazillu man waalayta tabaaraka rab-banaa wata'aalayta." **Al-turmizi**	"اللَّهُمَّ اهْدِنِي فِيمَنْ هَدَيْتَ، وَعَافِنِي فِيمَنْ عَافَيْتَ، وَتَوَلَّنِي فِيمَنْ تَوَلَّيْتَ، وَبَارِكْ لِي فِيمَا أَعْطَيْتَ، وَقِنِي شَرَّ مَا قَضَيْتَ، فَإِنَّكَ تَقْضِي وَلا يُقْضَى عَلَيْكَ، وَإِنَّهُ لا يَذِلُّ مَنْ وَالَيْتَ، تَبَارَكْتَ رَبَّنَا وَتَعَالَيْتَ" (الترمذي)	"O Allah! Guide me along with those whom You have guided, pardon me along with those whom You have pardoned, be my ally along with those of whom You are an ally, and bless that which You have bestowed on me, protect me from the evil You have decreed for verily, You decree, and none can decree over You. Surely, he whom You show allegiance to is never abased. O our Lord! Blessed and Exalted You are."

Supplications of sujuud of recitation

دُعاءُ سُجُودِ التِّلاوَةِ

No.	Transliteration	Arabic	English Meaning
1.	"Sajada wajhii lil-lazii khalaqahu wa shaq-qa sam'ahu wa basarahu bihawlihi waqudratihi fatabaaraka- llaahu ahsanu-l-khaaliqiin." **Al-Termizi & Ahmad**	"سَجَدَ وَجْهِي لِلَّذِي خَلَقَهُ وَشَقَّ سَمْعَهُ وَبَصَرَهُ بِحَوْلِهِ وَقُوَّتِهِ، فَتَبَارَكَ اللَّهُ أَحْسَنُ الخَالِقِينَ" (الترمذي وأحمد)	"My face fell prostrate before he who created it and brought forth its faculties of hearing and seeing by His might and power. So Blessed is Allah, the best of Creators." **At-Termizi & Ahmad**
2.	"Allahumma-ktub lii 'indaka bihaa ajran wa da' 'annii bihaa wizran waj'alhaa lii 'indaka zukhran wa taqab-balahaa minnii kamaa taqab-baltahaa min 'abdika Daawuud." **Al-Termizi & Al-Hakim**	"اللَّهُمَّ اكْتُبْ لِي عِنْدَكَ بِهَا أَجْرًا، وَضَعْ عَنِّي بِهَا وِزْرًا، وَاجْعَلْهَا لِي عِنْدَكَ ذُخْرًا، وَتَقَبَّلْهَا مِنِّي كَمَا تَقَبَّلْتَهَا مِنْ عَبْدِكَ دَاوُد" (الترمذي والحاكم)	"O Allah, for this prostration, credit me with a reward and wipe out a sin. Save it for me and accept it from me just as You had accepted it from Your servant Dawuud (David)." **At-Termizi & Al-Hakim**

Supplications after Salaat

أَذْكَارُ ما بَعْدَ الصَّلاةِ

No.	Transliteration	Arabic	English Meaning
1.	"Astaghfiru –llaah (3 times)"	أَسْتَغْفِرُ اللَّهَ (٣ مرَّاتٍ)	"I ask Allah for forgiveness (3 times)."
2.	"Allahum-ma anta-s-salaamu wa minka-s-salaamu tabaarakta yaa zal jalaali wal ikraam." **Muslim**	"اللَّهُمَّ أَنْتَ السَّلامُ وَمِنْكَ السَّلامُ، تَبَارَكْتَ يَاذا الجَلالِ والإكْرامِ" (مسلم)	"O Allah! You are Assalam, and from You comes all peace, Blessed You are, O Possessor of majesty and honor." **Muslim**
3.	"Laa ilaaha illa-llaahu wahdahu laa shariika lahu- lahu-l-mulku wa lahu-l-hamdu wahuwa 'alaa kulli shay^in qadiir Allahum-ma laa maani'a limaa a'tayta wa laa mu'tiya limaa mana'ta- wa laa yanfa'u zal jaddi minka-l-jadd." **Bukhari & Muslim**	"لا إِلَهَ إِلا اللَّهُ وَحْدَهُ لا شَرِيكَ لَهُ، لَهُ المُلْكُ وَلَهُ الحَمْدُ، يُحْيِي وَيُمِيتُ، وَهُوَ عَلَى كُلِّ شَيْءٍ قَدِيرٌ، اللَّهُمَّ لا مانِعَ لِمَا أَعْطَيْتَ ولا مُعْطِيَ لِما مَنَعْتَ، ولا يَنْفَعُ ذا الجَدِّ مِنْكَ الجَدُّ" (البخاري ومسلم)	"None has the right to be worshiped but Allah alone, without partner. To Him belongs all sovereignty and praise, and He is omnipotent over all things. O Allah! None can prevent what You have willed to bestow, and none can bestow what You have willed to prevent, and no wealth or majesty can benefit anyone, as from You is all wealth and majesty." **Bukhari & Muslim**
4.	"Subhaana-llaahi wa-l-hamud lillaahi wa-llaahu akbar (33 times)" **Muslim**	"سُبْحانَ اللهِ والحَمْدُ للهِ واللهُ أَكْبَرُ" ٣٣ مرَّةً (مسلم)	"How perfect Allah is. And all praise is for Allah. And Allah is greater (33 times)." **Muslim**
5.	Suurat al-Ikhlaas (3 marraat).	"سُورَةُ الإِخْلاصِ (٣ مرّاتٍ)	Suurat al-Ikhlas (112) 3 times.
6.	Suurat al-Falaq (3 marraat).	سُورَةُ الفَلَقِ (٣ مرّاتٍ)	Suurat al-Falaq (113) 3 times.
7.	Suurat an-nas (3 marraat).	سُورَةُ النَّاسِ (٣ مرّاتٍ)	Suruat al-Nass (113) 3 times.

Remember that there are many other authentic remembrances and supplications. Select and vary between them as it is the Sun-nah of the Prophet to vary between supplications.

Istikaarah Du'aa^

دُعَاءُ الاسْتِخَارَةِ

No.	Transliteration	Arabic	English Meaning
1.	"Allahumma astakhiiruka bi 'ilmika wa astaqdiruka bi qudratika wa as^aluka min fadlika-l-'aziim fa in-naka taqdiru wa laa aqdir wa ta'lamu wa laa A'lam Allahumma in kunta ta'lamu anna haaza-l-amra khayrun lii fii diinii wa ma'aashii wa 'aaqibati amrii fa-qdirhu lii wa yassirhu lii thumma baarik lii fiihi wa in kunta ta'alamu anna haaza-l-amra shar-run lii fii diinii wa ma'aashi wa 'aqibati amrii fa-srifuh 'anni wa-srifnii 'anhu waqdir liya-l-khayira haythu kaana- thum-ma ardinii bihi."	<div dir="rtl">اللَّهُمَّ اسْتَخِيرُكَ بِعِلْمِكَ وَاسْتَقْدِرُكَ بِقُدْرَتِكَ وَأَسْأَلُكَ مِنْ فَضْلِكَ الْعَظِيمِ ، فَإِنَّكَ تَقْدِرُ وَلَا أَقْدِرُ ، وَتَعْلَمُ وَلَا أَعْلَمُ. اللَّهُمَّ إِنْ كُنْتَ تَعْلَمُ أَنَّ هَذَا الْأَمْرَ خَيْرٌ لِي فِي دِينِي وَمَعَاشِي وَعَاقِبَةِ أَمْرِي فَاقْدُرْهُ لِي وَيَسِّرْهُ لِي ثُمَّ بَارِكْ لِي فِيهِ . وَإِنْ كُنْتَ تَعْلَمُ أَنَّ هَذَا الْأَمْرَ شَرٌّ لِي فِي دِينِي وَمَعَاشِي وَعَاقِبَةِ أَمْرِي فَاصْرِفْهُ عَنِّي وَاصْرِفْنِي عَنْهُ. وَاقْدُرْ لِي الْخَيْرَ حَيْثُ كَانَ . ثُمَّ أَرْضِنِي بِهِ.</div>	"O Allah! I consult You as You are the All-Knowing and I appeal to You to give me power as You are Omnipotent, I ask You for Your great favor, for You have power and I do not, and You know all matters but I do not. O Allah, if You know that this issue (name it) is best for me in my religion, my life, and for my Afterlife, facilitate it for me. But if you know that this issue (name it) is bad for me in my religion, my life and Afterlife, then keep it away from me and keep me away from it, and choose the best for me wherever it is and please me with it."

Supplicationof Funeral Salaat

دُعَاءُ صَلاةِ الجِنَازَةِ

No.	Transliteration	Arabic	English Meaning
1.	"Allaahumma-ghfir li-hayyinaa wa mayyitinaa wa li haadirinaa wa ghaa^ibinaa wa saghiirinaa wa kabiirinaa wa zakarinaa wa unthaanaa Allqahumma man ahyaytahu minna fa^ahiyhi 'alaa-l-islaam wa man tawaffaytahu minnaa fatawaffahu 'ala-l-imaan Allaahumma laa tahrimnaa ajrahu wa laa tudilanaa ba'dahu." **Ibn Maajah & Ahmad**	<div dir="rtl">اللَّهُمَّ اغْفِرْ لِحَيِّنَا وَمَيِّتِنَا، وَلِحَاضِرِنَا وَغَائِبِنَا، وَصَغِيرِنَا وَكَبِيرِنَا، وَذَكَرِنَا وَأُنْثَانَا، اللَّهُمَّ مَنْ أَحْيَيْتَهُ مِنَّا فَأَحْيِهِ عَلَى الإِسْلَامِ، وَمَنْ تَوَفَّيْتَهُ مِنَّا فَتَوَفَّهُ عَلَى الإِيمَانِ، اللَّهُمَّ لا تَحْرِمْنَا أَجْرَهُ وَلا تُضِلَّنَا بَعْدَهُ</div>	"O Allah! Forgive our living and our dead, those present and those absent, our young and our old, our males and our females. O Allah, whom amongst us You keep alive, then let such a life be with Islam, and whom amongst us You take unto Yourself, then let such a death be with faith. O Allah, do not deprive us of his reward and do not let us stray after him." **Ibn Maajah & Ahmad**

General Supplications

أَدْعِيَةٌ عَامَّةٌ

No.	Transliteration	Arabic	English Meaning
1.	**Sayyed al-Istighfaar** "Allahum-ma anta rab-bii laa ilaha illaa anta. Khalqtanii wa anaa 'abduka- wa anaa 'ala 'ahdika wa wa'dika ma-stata'tu abuu^u laka bini'matika 'alayya wa abuu^u bizanbii fa-ghfir lii innahu laa yaghfiru-z-zunuuba il-laa anta." **Al-turmizi**	<div dir="rtl">سَيِّدُ الاسْتِغْفَارِ</div> <div dir="rtl">"اللَّهُمَّ أَنْتَ رَبِّي لا إِلَهَ إِلَّا أَنْتَ، خَلَقْتَنِي وَأَنَا عَبْدُكَ، وَأَنَا عَلَى عَهْدِكَ وَوَعْدِكَ مَا اسْتَطَعْتُ، أَعُوذُ بِكَ مِنْ شَرِّ مَا صَنَعْتُ، أَبُوءُ لَكَ بِنِعْمَتِكَ عَلَيَّ، وَأَبُوءُ بِذَنْبِي، فَاغْفِرْ لِي، إِنَّهُ لا يَغْفِرُ الذُّنُوبَ إِلَّا أَنْتَ"</div>	The Master of forgiveness, Seeking: "O Allah! You are my Lord- There is no deity but You. You created me, and I am Your slave. And I am on Your covenant and promise as best as I can- I do acknowledge Your blessings on me. And I do confess of my sins. So, forgive me. There is no one to forgive sins but You."

What the Messenger Recited in His <u>S</u>alaats

One can recite any chapter or part of a chapter and can also repeat the same chapter in successive rak'ats. The most commonly used recitations of the Prophet are as follows:

The Five Obligatory <u>S</u>alaats

Fajr <u>S</u>alaat
Al-Fati<u>h</u>ah + any suurah from al-Fat<u>h</u> to an-Naba^

<u>Z</u>uhr <u>S</u>alaat
Al-Fati<u>h</u>ah + any suurah from an-Naba^ to ad-<u>D</u>uhaa

'Asr <u>S</u>alaat
Al-Fati<u>h</u>ah + any suurah from an-Naba^ to ad-<u>D</u>uhaa

Maghrib <u>S</u>alaat
Al-Fati<u>h</u>ah + any suurah from ad-<u>D</u>uhaa - an-Naas

Ishaa^ <u>S</u>alaat
Al-Fati<u>h</u>ah + any suurah from an-Naba^ to ad-<u>D</u>uhaa

Other <u>S</u>alaats

Friday <u>S</u>alaat
Al-Fati<u>h</u>ah + al- A'laa & al-Ghaashiyah
or al-Jumu'ah & al-Munaafiquun

'Eid <u>S</u>alaat
Al-Fati<u>h</u>ah + al-A'laa & al-Ghashiyah

Seeking Rain <u>S</u>alaat
Al-Fati<u>h</u>ah + al-A'laa & al-Ghasiyah

Funeral <u>S</u>alaat
Al-Fati<u>h</u>ah after the 1st takbiirah only

Seeking -Permission <u>S</u>alaat
Nothing specific

Eclipse <u>S</u>alaat
Al-Fati<u>h</u>ah + any long recitation such as al-Baqarah or aal-'imraan

Fear <u>S</u>alaat
Nothing specific

Sun-nah of Fajr <u>S</u>alaat
Al-Fati<u>h</u>ah + al-Kaafiruun & al-Ikhlaas
Or aayah 163 of al-baqarah & aayah 64 of aal-'imraan

Sun-nah of Maghrib <u>S</u>alaat
Al-Kaafiruun & al-Ikhlaas

Sun-nah of Witr <u>S</u>alaat
Al- A'laa + al-Kaafiruun + al-Ikhlaas

Night <u>S</u>alaat
Nothing Specific

Fajr of <u>F</u>riday <u>S</u>alaat
As-Sajdah & al-Insaan

A
B
C
D
E
F
G
H
I
J
K
L
M
N
O
P
Q
R
S
T
U
V
W
X
Y
Z

Washing Both Hands

Cleaning the Mouth

Inhaling Water through Nose

Washing the Face

Washing Both Arms

Wiping the Head

Wiping the Ears

Washing Both Feet

Facing the Qiblah

Takbiirat al-Ihram

Reciting the Qur'an

Making Rukuu'

Rising from Rukuu'

Making 1st Sujuud

Sitting after 1st Sujuud

Making 2nd Sujuud

Rising from Sujuud

Beginning 2nd Rak'ah

Making Rukuu'

Rising from Rukuu'

Making 1st Sujuud

Sitting after 1st Sujuud

Making 2nd Sujuud

Sitting for Tashah-hud

Sitting for Last Tashah-hud

Making Tasliim

Section Four
Other Salaats

Other Salaats

Introduction

As clearly presented in the first few chapters, Salaat is the essence of worshiping Almighty Allah. It is a prescribed way to show love, respect, submission, and obedience to Him. No wonder it is the most important pillar of Islam. Not only do Muslims perform the five obligatory Salaats, but they also perform other significant Salaats as well. This section is solely dedicated to these Salaats.

In an attempt to make this book more inclusive, most of these Salaats, which have different rulings, have been integrated. Some of these Salaats are collective, while others are individual Salaats, some are both. From another facet, some of these Salaats are more common than others. From a third perspective, some Salaats are communal, which means that they should be performed by some, not by all Muslims, such as Jinazah Salaat.

It is worth mentioning that not all other Salaats are covered in this book. Only the most authentic ones, which are not disputed among scholars, have been addressed. For example, since the tasbiih Salaat is quite debatable among scholars it has been left out. Sadly enough, some of these Salaats, i.e. eclipse Salaat, are abandoned by some Muslims. Although it is an authentic Sun-nah to perform these Salaats collectively and individually, many Muslims ignore it. Performing such prayers is very significant. It is a clear proof that people glorify Allah with submission and respect. In His own words, He reminded us by saying:

﴿ ذَٰلِكَ وَمَن يُعَظِّمْ شَعَـٰٓئِرَ ٱللَّهِ فَإِنَّهَا مِن تَقْوَى ٱلْقُلُوبِ ﴾
الحج: ٣٢

"That (is the command): Whoever glorifies the commands of Allah, it surely is from the devotion of the hearts." **(22:32)**. Undoubtedly, there are great rewards in reviving the traditions of the Messenger of Allah (pbuh).

In this section, I listed the most common salaats. Friday Salaat is a common Salaat, which renders great rewards and blessings. For example, it can be the cause of erasing ones sins from one Friday to the next. A less commonly performed Salaat is the Salaat of Fear. It is the Salaat that is done only at times when one is in a state of danger or fear. Although it is an emphasized Sun-nah of the Messenger of Allah (pbuh), it is one of the least frequently offered Salaats.

1. Salaat of the Traveler
2. Salaat of the Ill
3. Friday Salaat
4. Eiid Salaat
5. Night Salaat
6. Tarawiih Salaat
7. Witr Salaat
8. Eclipse Salaat
9. Istisqaaˆ Salaat
10. Fear Salaat
11. Jinaazah Salaat
12. Istikharah Salaat

I would like to remind the readers that the layout of this section is slightly different from the A-to-Z section due to unique nature of these Salaats. Finally, I hope that this book becomes a strong reminder for Muslims worldwide to perform such important Salaats.

Salaat of the Traveler

Definition: It is a privilege given to any traveler to shorten and (combine) Salaats together.

Ruling: It is one of the most emphasized sun-nah.

When: From the time the traveler leaves his residence until he comes back.

Where: Anywhere as long as it is clean.

Who: It can be done collectively or individually.

Conditions:

❶ It should be performed only during the actual time of traveling.

❷ One should pray towards the direction of the Ka'bah.

❸ Neither Maghrib Salaat nor the Fajr Salaat is shortened.

❹ Travelers are not obligated to perform Jumu'ah Salaat.

❺ It can be days, months, or even years; as long as some one is in a state of travel.

Description:

A traveler can shorten the long prayers: Zhur, 'Asr, and 'Ishaaˆ. Instead of making 4 rak'ahs, the traveler offers two rak'ahs. They should be performed like any regular Salaat.

Recommended Issues:

❶ It is recommended to be in congregation.

❷ It is recommended not to combine two Salaats together unless a person is actually traveling.

❸ It is not recommended for a traveler to do voluntary Salaats except for Fajr sun-nah and Witr sun-nah.

❹ It is recommended to combine Zhur and 'Asr at the time of Zhur; and Maghrib and 'Ishaaˆ at the time of 'Ishaaˆ.

❺ On traveling it is recommended to make this du'aaˆ: اللهُ اكْبَرُ – اللهُ اكْبَرُ – اللهُ اكْبَرُ

"سُبْحانَ الَّذي سَخَّرَ لَنا هَذا وَما كُنَّا لَهُ مُقْرِنِينَ وَإِنَّا إِلَى رَبِّنا لَمُنْقَلِبُونَ."

اللَّهُمَّ إِنَّا نَسْأَلُكَ في سَفَرِنا هَذا البِرَّ والتَّقْوَى، وَمِنَ العَمَلِ ما تَرْضَى،

اللَّهُمَّ هَوِّنْ عَلَيْنا سَفَرَنا هَذا وَاطْوِ عَنَّا بُعْدَهُ ، اللَّهُمَّ أَنْتَ الصّاحِبُ في السَّفَرِ والخَلِيفَةُ في الأهْلِ،

اللَّهُمَّ إِنِّي أَعُوذُ بِكَ مِنْ وَعْثاءِ السَّفَرِ وكَآبَةِ المَنْظَرِ وسُوءِ المُنْقَلَبِ في المالِ والأهْلِ."

Al-Musafir Salaat صَلاةُ المُسافِرِ

Evidence:
❶ Ibn 'Ab-baas (ra) narrated that the Messenger of Allah continued to shorten his Salaats for more than 90 days. **Al-Bukhari**

Common Errors:
❶ Shortening Maghrib Salaat to two rak'ahs.

Questions & Answers

Q1 What is the ruling on combining 2 Salaats at one time?

A It is an emphasized sun-nah.

Q2 Can one combine 2 Salaats for reasons other than traveling?

A Yes, at times of sickness, it is permissible to combine Salaats.

Q3 What if a traveler prays behind an imaam who is resident? Should the traveler complete or shorten his Salaats?

A He should complete them. He has to follow the imaam. However, if the imaam is the traveler he will shorten his prayer and the ma^muum will complete the first Salaat.

Q4 How can one perform Salaat on a ship or an airplane or in an automobile?

A When one begins the Salaat one stands up to face the direction of the Qiblah. If this is not possible, one is permitted to sit on chair and perform it as if one is ill.

Golden Tip:
❶ The travelers du'aaˆ is very special. It is always accepted. So, increase your du'aa as much as you can while traveling.

Imaam
Like any of the five daily Salaats.

Maˆmuum
Like any of the five daily Salaats.

Individual
Like any of the five daily Salaats.

Males
No difference.

Females
No difference.

Salaat of the Ill

Definition: It is a privilege given to any one who is in a state of sickness, in which he/she is allowed to make Salaat while sitting or lying on his/her side or back or anyway that is comfortable to him/her.

Ruling: It is one of the most emphasized sun-nah.

When: As long as the person is in a state of sickness, no matter how long it is.

Where: In bed, in a chair, or at any place.

Who: Applicable only for people who are sick.

Conditions:

❶ Only during the actual period of illness.

❷ One should make an effort to pray towards the direction of the Ka'bah.

❸ It can be done collectively or individually.

❹ It can be days, months, or even years; as long as some one is in a state of illness.

Description:

An ill person can pray in a chair. It is better to begin Salaat while standing, then a person can sit down. If you perform the Salaat while sitting, bend forward in case of rukuu'. In case of sujuud, bend further down more forward. If you cannot bend, nod by your neck. If you cannot, use you eyelids or move your hand. The most important thing is not to miss the Salaat for any reason.

Recommended Issues:

❶ It is recommended to be in congregation (if possible).

❷ It is recommended to use the most comfortable way.

❸ It is recommended to do the voluntary Salaats (if possible).

❹ An ill person can combine two Salaats together.

❺ If you cannot make wuduuˆ, make tayam-mum.

Salaat al-Mariid  صَلاةُ المَرِيضِ

Evidence:

❶ 'Imran ibn Hussain (ra) narrated that: "I had hemorrhoids. Then I asked the Messenger of Allah about Salaat. He said: *"Pray standing. If you cannot, pray sitting. If you cannot' pray on your side."* **Al-Bukhari**

Common Errors:

❶ Postponing the Salaat until the ill person recovers.

❷ Shortening the 4 rak'ahs to 2 rak'ahs.

Questions & Answers

Ⓠ① Can a person combine two Salaats together because of illness?

Ⓐ Yes, he can.

Ⓠ② What are other situations in which a person can combine Salaats?

Ⓐ A person can combine Salaats together in case of traveling, illness, rain, snow, etc.

Ⓠ③ How can a person pray while he is an operation room?

Ⓐ If there is no way of making wuduu or tayam-mum, he can pray without any of these forms of ablution.

Ⓠ④ If a person lost consciousness for some hours or days, should he make up for the missed Salaats when he wakes up?

Ⓐ Yes, he has to make up for all missed Salaats.

Golden Tip:

❶ Remember that if you are patient with your illness, it is a cause to erase your sins. So, be patient and make more du'aaˆ.

Imaam
Like any of the five daily Salaats.

Maˆmuum
Like any of the five daily Salaats.

Individual
Like any of the five daily Salaats.

Males
No difference.

Females
No difference.

Friday Salaat

Definition: It is a Salaat that is held once a week on Friday.

Ruling: It is obligatory on males

When: The same time of Zuhr Salaat. There is no harm if it begins before meridian of the sun.

Where: Any place, whether it is a masjid, a hall, a building, or a park. It can be performed in more than one place in the same city.

Who: Every free, sane, adult Muslim. Women can perform Jumu'ah Salaat. However, it is preferred for women to pray at home. In this case żuhr prayer.

Conditions:
❶ It is a congregational Salaat not an individual one.
❷ Thus, a group of as few as three people is enough for holding it.
❸ People should be resident. (Travelers can perform Zuhr instead of Friday Salaat).
❹ Friday khutbah is obligatory.

Description of Khutbah:
❶ The khutbah consists of 2 parts. Between them, the imaam sits down briefly.
❷ The imaam should greet the audience with (Assalaamu Alaykum Wa Rahmatu-llaahi wa barakaatuhu).
❸ The khutbahs include praise of the Almighty Allah, Salaats unto the Messenger, a spiritual sermon, and Qur'anic recitations.
❹ The imaam stands while delivering the two khutbahs.
❺ The khutbahs should be short and audible to the audience.
❻ The khutbahs should be before the Salaat.

Description of Friday Salaat:
❶ It consists of two rak'ahs.
❷ The recitation should be aloud.
❸ It is strongly recommended to read suurat al-A'laa in the 1st rak'at, and suurat al-Ghaashiyah in the 2nd. However, it is permissible to read other suurahs.

Importance: Friday is the best day of the week.

Recommended Issues:
❶ Reciting suurah al-Kahf is strongly recommended on Friday by night or day.
❷ It is also recommended to send many salutations to the Messenger (peace be unto him).
❸ It is recommended to take a shower (ghusl) before the Salaat.
❹ It is also recommended for men to wear perfume and the best attire.
❺ It recommended to be at the masjid early to get more reward.

Jumu'ah Salaat

صَلاَةُ الجُمُعَةِ

Evidence:

1. The Messenger Muhammad (pbuh) used to offer Jumu'ah Salaat every Friday. **By consensus**

Common Errors:

1. Coming late to masjids and missing parts of the khutbah.
2. Sleeping during the khutbah.
3. Speaking during the khutbah.
4. Stepping over people to reach the front rows.
5. Some imaams prolong the khutbahs.

Questions & Answers

Q1 Can one perform Salaat al-Zhur after Friday Salaat?

A No. If one performs Friday Salaat, the Żuhr Salaat is dropped.

Q2 What happens if a person does not catch up with the rukuu' of the 2nd rak'ah?

A One should complete the Salaat with the imaam and should then complete four rak'ahs as a Żuhr Salaat.

Q3 If one arrives while the imaam is delivering the khutbah, should one sit or do two rak'ahs?

A One should do two brief rak'ahs.

Q4 Is it permissible for women to attend

A Yes, it is permissible but not obligatory.

Q5 What is the ruling on some mosques where a reciter recites the Qur'an while the rest of people listen before Friday Salaat?

A This is not the sun-nah of the Messenger of Allah. The sun-nah is that each one recites the Qur'an individually.

Golden Tip:

1. Friday is the best day of the week. It has many bounties. Triple your supplications on that day, especially the last hour before sunset. During this hour, Almighty Allah responds to supplications. So, take advantage of that.

Imaam
Like any audible Salaat.

Maˆmuum
Like any audible Salaat.

Individual
Like any audible Salaat.

Males
No difference.

Females
No difference.

Definition: It is a <u>S</u>alaat that is held at Eiidu-l-Fitr and at Eiidu-l-Adhaa.

Ruling: It is Fard Kifaayah (communal obligation). It is not obligatory for every Muslim. It is sufficient to be performed by some Muslims.

When: From the time the sun is a spear's height above the horizon until the sun reaches its zenith.

Where: ❶ It is performed in open space outside the city unless it is not possible except in a masjid.
❷ It is recommended to arrange it at one place per town/city in order to gather the maximum number of Muslims in one place.

Who: Muslims: males, females and children.

Conditions:

❶ The <u>S</u>alaat is made without A<u>z</u>aan or Iqaamah.
❷ It is not recommended to pray any sun-nah before or after Eiid <u>S</u>alaat.

Description of Khutbah:

The khutbah is after the <u>S</u>alaat. It is a sun-nah to attend the khutbah. It begins with praising the Almighty Allah. It includes a sermon and teaches people specifics relevant to each Eid.

Description of <u>S</u>alaat:

❶ It consists of two rak'ahs.
❷ In the 1st, the imaam announces takbiiratu-l-ihraam + 6 more takbiirahs. (he raises the two hands in each of them).
❸ After 7 takbiirahs, he recites al-Fatiha and a suurah, preferably al-A'laa..

❹ He continues like any regular <u>S</u>alaat.
❺ In the 2nd rak'ah, he makes 5 takbiirahs in addition to the takbiirah of standing up from sujuud. (He raises the two hands in each of them).
❻ Then he recites al-Fatiha and a suurah, preferably al-Ghaashiyah.

Recommended Issues:

❶ It is recommended to announce takbiir on the 2 Eiids.
❷ On Eiidu-l-Fitr, from the sunset of the last day of Ramadan until the <u>S</u>alaat of Eiid starts. As for Eiidu-l-Adhaa, takbiir is recommended from the 1st day of Thul-Hijjah until the Maghrib of the 13th day. There is also special takbiir after the obligatory <u>S</u>alaats from the Fajr of the day of 'Arafat until the Asr of the 13th of Thul-Hijjah.
❸ It is recommended to take a shower and be in the best attire.
❹ It is recommended to go from one way and come from the other.
❺ Menstruating women are encouraged to witness the Eiid but they avoid being in the <u>S</u>alaat area.

Eiid Salaat صَلاةُ العِيدِ

Evidence:

❶ Ibn 'Umar (ra) narrated that:
"The Messenger of Allah, Abu Bakr and 'Umar used to pray the Salaat of the two Eiids before the khutbah." **Agreed upon**

Questions & Answers

1 Is it permissible for women to attend Eiid Salaats?

A Indeed, it is very much recommended to attend Eiid, even when menstruating. They should avoid the Salaat area.

2 What if one arrives for the Salaat after the rukuu' of the 2nd rak'ah?

A One should complete it as Salaat Eiid in the above explained manner.

4 When should the opening supplication be recited?

A It is possible to recite it either before or after the takbiirahs.

5 What if the imaam forgets the takbiirahs.

A The Salaat is correct because the additional takbiirahs are sun-nah.

6 What is the ruling on collectively announced takbiir before the Salaat?

A The Sun-nah of the Messenger of Allah is to announce it individually. Men are also recommended to do it aloud.

Common Errors:

❶ Not accompanying family members to attend Eiid.

❷ Not articulating takbiir.

❸ Repeating the takbiirs collectively.

❹ Delaying Zakaat al-Fitr until the Salaat is established.

❺ Slaughtering the sacrifice of al-Adha Eiid before the end of the Eiid Al-Adha Salaat.

Golden Tip:

❶ This is the day of Eiid. So, express your love to others, and share your happiness with them. Do your best to make everyone happy; your parents, kids, spouses, friends and neighbors. Do not forget the poor. Make them smile.

Imaam
Like any audible Salaat.

Ma^muum
Like any audible Salaat.

Individual
Like any audible Salaat.

Males
No difference.

Females
No difference.

Definition: It is a <u>S</u>alaat that is performed after 'Ishaa^ <u>S</u>alaat but before witr and can be observed all year round.

Ruling: It is a recommended sun-nah which the Messenger never missed even during travel.

When: It is performed after Ishaa^ <u>S</u>alaat.

Where: Anywhere but it is better to be performed at home.

Who: Every adult, sane, male and female Muslim.

Conditions:

❶ It is performed individually.

❷ It is also done collectively during Ramadan after taraawiih <u>S</u>alaat.

❸ It can also be done collectively provided that it is not done consistently.

Description:

It is like any other <u>S</u>alaat except that the recitations are preferred to be longer than usual. It is possible to repeat the suurahs or the aayahs in the same, and in the following rak'ahs.

Content: One can read any 2 surahs in the 3 rak'ahs. However, the Messenger used to select long surahs.

Recommended Issues:

❶ It is recommended to do it after midnight but before dawn (sahar).

❷ It is better to perform fewer and longer rak'ahs rather than many rak'ahs.

❸ It can be done silently or aloud.

The Night Salaat

Evidence:

① 'Abdullahi Ibn 'Amru (ra) narrated that the messenger of Allah (pbuh) said:
"The best of fasting is the fasting of Dawuud's, and the best of Salaats to Allah is the Salaat of Dawuud. He used to sleep half of the night, and pray one third, and sleep one sixth; and he used to fast every other day." **Agreed upon**

Questions & Answers

①Q Is it possible to do more than 13 rak'ahs including witr Salaat?

A Yes, and the evidence comes from the hadiith of Ibn 'Umar (ra). **Agreed upon.**

②Q What is the best time to do the night Salaat?

A In general, the last portion of the night is better than the first, unless one might fear not being able to get up at night. In this case, one can do it in the first part of the night.

③Q Can I do 4 rak'ahs in one Salaat?

A No. The sun-nah is 2 rak'ahs every Salaat.

④Q Can I do the night Salaat with my family?

A Yes, it is permissible.

⑤Q Should the Salaat be audible or silent?

A It can be either. What really matters is to gain khushuu' through Salaat.

Common Errors:

① Some people don't benefit from these night prayers.

② Some people make it 4 rak'ahs at a time (instead of two).

Golden Tip:

① The night Salaat has a special taste and reward. Offering Salaat in the middle of the night while others are asleep has a great impact on people's hearts. It softens their hearts and truly guides them to enjoy the beauty of worship.

Imaam
Ma^muum
Individual

The night Salaat is always done individually, unless it is in Ramadan, it is called Tarawiih

Males
No difference.

Females
No difference.

Taraawiih Salaat

Definition: It is a Salaat that is performed during the month of Ramadan after 'Ishaaˆ Salaat.

Ruling: It is an emphasized sun-nah for men and women, which the Messenger (pbuh) performed for three nights in the mosque, and the rest of nights he performed at home. He did that lest it might become an obligation for Muslims.

When: It is done after Ishaaˆ Salaat.

Where: Usually it is performed in masjids in congregation but it can be done elsewhere.

Who: Every adult, sane, male and female Muslim.

Conditions:
❶ It is performed collectively or individually.

Description:
❶ It is performed two rak'ahs at a time, in congregation like any other two rak'ahs.
❷ The recitation is longer than usual.
❸ The authentic number of rak'ahs is 11 including witr. However, one can add more rak'ahs.
❹ It is preferable to take a rest between every four rakahs.
❺ It usually ends with qunuut du'aaˆ either before or after the rukuu' of the last rak'ah.

Content: It is preferred to prolong the recitation in each of the 2 rak'ahs one can read Al-Fatihah + any verse.

Recommended Issues:
❶ One is recommended to do it after 'Ishaaˆ Salaat.
❷ One is recommended to take some rest between every four rak'ahs, following the imaam.
❸ One is recommended to make du'aaˆ qunuut in the Witr Salaat.
❹ One is recommended to follow and finish with the imaam, not before, regardless of how many rak'ahs the imaam does.
❺ One is recommended to recite the entire Qur'an during the month.
❻ One is recommended to come to masjid early to pray Ishaaˆ Salaat in congregation before the beginning of taraawiih.

Taraawiih Salaat

Evidence:

1. 'Abu Zar (ra) narrated that the messenger of Allah (pbuh) said that: "Whoever prays with the imaam until he finishes Salaat, it will be counted as one night (of Salaat)." **Agreed upon**

Questions & Answers

Q1 What is the number of rak'ahs in taraawiih Salaat?

A The sun-nah of the Messenger of Allah is 11 or 13 rak'ahs. However, it is permissible to perform more rak'ahs. Remember that this issue should not be a cause for dispute among Muslims.

Q2 How long should it take?

A The sun-nah of the Messenger (pbuh) is that it is usually longer than the regular Salaat. However, it should not be too long so that it becomes hard for most people nor too short, so that it makes people miss the sunan during the Salaat.

Q3 Some people care for taraawiih Salaat more than obligatory ones. What is the ruling on this act?

A Nothing pleases Allah more than doing the obligatory Salaats. Therefore, people should be more keen on doing the Fajr Salaat than taraawiih Salaats. But, if they can do both, that is much better.

Q4 What if one misses Ishaaˆ Salaat and then comes to the masjid and sees the congregation doing taraawiih Salaat?

A One can join the taraawiih Salaat with the intention of Ishaaˆ Salaat.

Q5 What is the ruling regarding people who carry the mushaf while the imam is reciting?

A It is permissible for the imam to read from the mushaf, if there is a need for that. But the maˆmuum should not carry the mushaf unless one is using it to correct the imam.

Common Errors:

1. Leaving the masjid before the imaam finishes the whole tarawiih Salaats.
2. Some people carry mushafs for no need.
3. Some imaams prolong qunuut du'aaˆ excessively.
4. Some people make it very quickly.

Golden Tip:

1. Ramadan is a season of change. The intensity of worship in this particular month plays a great role in their life. Fasting, praying, making supplications make many positive changes in the Islamic identity. It is only once a year. Do not miss it.

Imaam
Maˆmuum
Individual
Like any audible Salaat.

Males
No difference.

Females
No difference.

Witr Salaat

Definition: It is a Salaat that is performed after Ishaa ˆ Salaat. It should have an odd number of rak'ats, i.e. (1/3/5/7/9/11)

Ruling: It is an emphasized sun-nah.

When: It is preferred to be done at the end of night Salaat.

Where: It may be performed anywhere.

Who: Every adult, sane, male and female Muslim.

Conditions:

❶ Normally, it is done individually but it can be done collectively.

❷ One cannot do it twice in one night. (No two witrs in one night).

Description:

If one does it 3 rak'ahs, one can do it in any form:

❶ 3 joint rak'ahs without sitting for tashah-hud after two rak'ahs.

❷ 2 separate rak'ahs followed by a 3rd separate one.

Content: One can read any three suurahs in the three rak'ahs. However, the Messenger (pbuh) used to do it in the following manner:

❶ In the 1st rak'ah, suurat al-Fatihah + surat al-A'laa

❷ In the 2nd rak'ah, suurat al-Fatihah + surat al-Kaafiruun

❸ In the 3rd rak'ah, suurat al-Fatihah+ surat al-ikhlaas

Recommended Issues:

❶ One is recommended to do it at the end of night Salaats unless one fears not being able to get up at night. Then do it after the sun-nah of Salaat al'shaa.

Witr Ṣalaat صَلاةُ الوِترِ

Evidence:

 Ibn 'Umar (ra) narrated that the Messenger of Allah (pbuh) said:
"End your Ṣalaats at night by an odd Ṣalaat (Witr)." **Agreed upon**

② Talq ibn 'Ali narrated that he heard the Messenger of Allah saying that:
"There should be no two witr Ṣalaats in one night." **Abu Dawuud, Termizi & Ibn Majah**

Questions & Answers

1 Q Is the qunuut in the witr Ṣalaat waajib?

A No. It is not. But doing it in the congregation in Ramadan is good. However, it is wise for the imaam to skip it some nights lest some people might think it is waajib.

2 Q If one gets up to do Fajr but misses the Witr Ṣalaat, how can one make up for it?

A One can make up for it at duhaa time by doing it in an even number instead of an odd number. This can be done by adding one rak'ah more than the usual number one is used to.

3 Q If one intends to perform tahaj-jud in the latter part of the night, should he do the witr with the imaam before leaving the masjid?

A One can do the witr with the imaam but instead of finishing with tasliim one stands to add one more rak'ah and, then, can do witr in the last part of the night.

4 Q What is the minimum rak'ahs for witr Ṣalaat?

A One rak'ah.

5 Q What if one does witr Ṣalaat then gets up at night. What can one do?

A One can do 2 rak'ahs at a time until one finishes. One does not have to do another witr.

6 Q How can one raise the hands in qunuut supplication?

A Bring the hands together parallel to you face, but not above the head.

Common Errors:

① Missing it by oversleeping.

② Making two witrs in one night.

Golden Tip:

① It is common to see people die while sleeping. So, a wise person does not want to sleep without offering this emphasized Ṣalaat. It might be the last Ṣalaat in one's life.

Imaam
Maˆmuum
Individual

Like any audible Ṣalaat if it is done in congregation. Otherwise, it will be like any individual sun-nah.

Males
No difference.

Females
No difference.

Eclipse Ṣalaat

Definition: It is a Ṣalaat that is performed whenever there is a Lunar or a Solar eclipse, full or partial.

Ruling: It is the most emphasized sun-nah. Some scholars see it as a waajib because the Messenger of Allah said: "Whenever you see the (eclipse) recite du'aaˆ, do takbiir, perform Ṣalaat, and pay charity.

When: From the time the eclipse begins until the eclipse ends.

Where: Anywhere as long as it is clean.

Who: It can be done collectively or individually.

Conditions:
❶ Only during the actual time of the eclipse.
❷ One should direct oneself towards the Ka'bah.
❸ The Ṣalaat of lunar eclipse and solar eclipse is exactly the same.

Description: It consists of two rak'ahs with two rukuu's in each.
❶ After reading the Fatiḥah, long recitation from the Qur'an should follow.
❷ Do takbiir then a long rukuu'.
❸ Rise from rukuu' and say: (Sami' Allahu liman hamidah) then recite the Fatiḥa and a long recitation from the Qur'an, which is shorter than the 1st one.
❹ Do takbiir then long rukuu', which should be shorter than the 1st rukuu'.
❺ Perform two long sujuuds, (as long as the rukuu's). In the 2nd rak'ah, do exactly the same. In all, there are 4 rukuu's and 4 sujuuds. In general, the 2nd rak'ah should be shorter than the 1st. Bear in mind, that these rak'ahs should be longer than in any regular Ṣalaat.

Recommended Issues:
❶ It is recommended to reflect upon the eclipse as an aayah (sign) from Allah to remind His servants of His power.
❷ If the Ṣalaat ends before the end of the eclipse and the imaam is recommended to deliver a speech until the Sun or Moon disappears. This, however, is not necessary.
❸ If the eclipse ends during Ṣalaat, the imaam should end it quickly.
❹ It is recommended to repeat the tasbiiḥ during the rukuu'.

Salaat al-Khusuuf صَلاةُ الخُسُوفِ

Evidence:

1 'Aishaa (ra) narrated that the Messenger of (pbuh) said: "*Indeed the sun and the moon and two signs from Allah. The eclipse of the sun or the moon does not take place because of the death or life of someone. So, if you see that (eclipse) make du'aaˆ, make takbiir, and pay charity, and make Salaat until the eclipse ends.*" **Agreed upon**

Common Errors:

1 Looking at the moon or sun during Salaat.

2 Continuing the Salaat even if the eclipse ends.

Questions & Answers

 Is one misses the 1st or the 2nd rukuu', does one have to redo the whole rak'ah?

A Yes.

2 What should one say when rising from the 1st rukuu'?

A Say: "Sami' Allahu liman hamidah".

3 Can I do 4 rak'ahs in one Salaat?

A No. The sun-nah is 2 rak'ahs every Salaat.

4 Should the Fatihah be recited after rising from 1st rukuu'?

A Not necessarily, because the Fatihah has already been recited before the 1st rukuu' (which is the pillar).

5 Does the eclipse Salaat require Azaan and Iqaamah?

A No. But the call for it is: (the congregational Salaat is called for)

الصَّلاةُ جامِعةٌ

This call can be repeated many times to inform people.

6 If one misses the time of eclipse, can Salaat be made up??

A No. The eclipse Salaat has to be done only during the time of actual eclipse.

Golden Tip:

1 The phenomenon of eclipse is a sign from Allah which shows His Might over the whole universe. Muslims show their gratitude to their Powerful Lord by submitting to Him during the time of eclipse. So, do not miss this opportunity.

Imaam
Maˆmuum
Individual

Like any audible Salaat. It can be done in congregation as well as individually.

Males
No difference.

Females
No difference.

Definition: It is a Salaat that is held whenever there is a shortage of rain or during droughts.

Ruling: It is an emphasized sun-nah.

When: Anytime except during the prohibited times (sunrise, sunset, and when the sun reaches its meridian).

Where: The sun-nah is to perform it out of the city but it can be done anywhere.

Who: Collectively.

Conditions:

❶ It has only one khutbah.
   The khutbah can either be before or after Salaat. But it is preferable to be before.

Description:

It is performed exactly as Eiid Salaat; 6 takbiirahs in the 1st rak'ah and 5 in the 2nd. The only difference is that the khutbah can either be before or after the Salaat. It is a two- rak'ah Salaat, and the recitation should be audible. In the 1st rak'at, the imam reads the al-Fatihah+ al-A'laa. In the 2nd rak'at, he reads al-Fatihah + al-Ghaashiyah. After the khutbah, it is recommended to raise one's hand while reciting seeking rain supplications. Here is one such supplication:

Supplication:

"All praise is for Allah, the Compassionate, the Merciful, the King of the Day of Judgment. There is no deity but Allah Who does what He wishes. O Allah, there is no deity but You. You are the Self-sufficient and we are the poor. Send down rain upon us and make it a source of strength and satisfaction for us."

الحَمْدُ لِلّهِ رَبِّ العالَمِينَ الرَّحْمَنِ الرَّحِيمِ مالِكِ يَوْمِ الدِّينِ

لا إِلَهَ إِلاَّ اللّهُ يَفْعَلُ ما يُرِيدُ

اللّهُمَّ لا إِلَهَ إِلاَّ أَنْتَ أَنْتَ الغَنِيُّ وَنَحْنُ الفُقَرَاءُ.

أَنْزِلْ عَلَيْنا الغَيْثَ واجْعَلْ ما أَنْزَلْتَ عَلَيْنا

قُوَّةً وَبَلاغًا إِلَى حِينٍ.

Recommended Issues:

❶ During the khutbah, the imaam recites istighfaar and du'aaˆ. It is recommended that the imaam and maˆmuums invert their cloaks as the Messenger (pbuh) did.

❷ It is also recommended that the rain-seeking supplications be offered in Friday Salaat as well.

Istisqaa^ Salaat

صَلاةُ الاسْتِسْقاءِ

Evidence:

❶ Abu Hurairah (ra) narrated that: *"Once the Messenger of Allah went out to make Istisqaa^ Salaat. He prayed two rak'ahs; the recitation was audible. There was no Azaan nor Iqaamah. Then he delivered a speech in which he pleaded to Almighty Allah. Then he turned his face towards Qiblah while raising his two hands. Then he inverted his cloak; he put the right side on the left and the left on the right side."* **Ahmad**

Questions & Answers

 Q How should the hands be during the du'aa^ outside Salaat?

A They should be close to each other and should be raised up high above the head.

 Q Is it better for women to attend this Salaat in congregation or at home?

A In congregation, because this is a collective Salaat, not an individual one.

 Q What if it rains, just before the time of Salaat?

A There will be no reason for Salaat.

 Q Should the listeners of the khutbah raise their hands when the imaam raises his?

A Yes, they should.

 Q How many times should Salaat be performed if the drought continues?

A It can be done many times. There is no limit.

Common Errors:

❶ Some people do not attend this Salaat out of laziness.

❷ Some people think that it should be done once a year.

Golden Tip:

❶ Allah loves those who show him humbleness and submission. Therefore, go to the prayer showing submission to Allah. This might trigger His mercy.

Imaam
Ma^muum
Individual

Like any audible Salaat.
It is done in congregation.

Males & Females

The only difference is that females do not invert their clothes.

Fear Salaat

Definition: It is a Salaat which is performed when one is in a state of fear of danger.

Ruling: It is permissible.

When: During a state of fear.

Where: Any clean place away from the source of danger.

Who: It should be done collectively.

Conditions:

❶ Only during the state of fear, danger or threat.

Description: It consists of two rak'ahs. It has many forms.
The following is the most common form:

❶ The imaam begins with group A while group B is guarding the back of group A.

❷ The imaam finishes the 1st rak'ah with group A but remains standing ready for the 2nd rak'ah while group A continues the 2nd rak'ah and finishes by performing tasliim without the imaam.

❸ Of course, the imaam is required to do a lengthy 2nd rak'at, in order to allow group B to catch up with him.

❹ Then group A takes the place of group B in guarding. While the imaam is still standing, group B stands behind him.

❺ The imaam finishes his 2nd rak'ah with group B.

❻ When the imaam sits for tashahhud, group B stands to do their 2nd rak'ah, while the imaam remains sitting in a lengthy tashah-hud and waiting.

❼ Group B sits for tashah-hud with the imaam.

❽ When the imaam performs tasliim, group B does the same.

Recommended Issues:

❶ It is recommended to do the above-mentioned form if the enemy is in the direction of the Qiblah. However, during the actual fighting or being chased by the enemy, one can do Salaat by oneself in any position. For example, one is allowed to pray by nodding while walking, riding, or running.

Khawf Salaat

صَلاةُ الخَوْفِ

Evidence:

❶ The Holy Qur'an stated the evidence of Salaat al-khawf in this verse: *"When you are among them, and lead them in Salaat, let one party of them stand up with you taking their arms with them: when they finish their prostrations, let them take their positions in the rear and let the other party come up which has not yet prayed and let them pray with you taking all the precautions and bearing arms."* **4: 102**

Questions & Answers

1 Q What is the wisdom behind Salaat al-khawf?

A First, Salaat is so essential that it cannot be dropped under any circumstances. Second, it shows Islam's practicality for all circumstances. Third, it tells us how valuable the human life is. One should be fully protected during time of danger. Fourth, it implies that ijtihaad is not allowed when a text exists. That is, no one can invent a form of 'ibaadah with the presence of a text from the Qur'an or the Sun-nah. Fifth, it shows importance the Sun-nah of the Messenger of Allah. Sixth, it is a proof for the importance of the congregational Salaat.

2 Q What is the proof for the authenticity of (Salaat al-khawf)?

A The Qur'anic verse in suurah **(4: 102)**, which commands Muslims to perform this Salaat.

3 Q Which group is better: A or B?

A Both are equal. Group A attends the takbiirat al-ihraam with the imaam but group B attends the tasliim.

4 Q During the Salaat al-khawf, can one hold one's weapons?

A Yes, he can.

Common Errors:

❶ Some people think that it should be done only at the time of war.

❷ Some people delay the Salaat instead of performing Salaat al-khawf.

Golden Tip:

❶ This Salaat shows a fair balance in this religion. Although the human life is very valuable and it should be protected by all means, at the same time Allah's commands should be obeyed by offering Salaat in congregation even during the time of danger.

Imaam & Ma^muum

The imaam prays 2 rakahs with 2 different groups whereas each ma^muum prays one rak'ah with the imaam & another rak'ah by himself.

Individual

The individual does not independently perform this form of Salaat.

Males & Females

Women are not obligated to perform it.

Funeral Salaat

Definition: It is a Salaat that is done for a deceased Muslim, male or female except the martyrs for whom there is no funeral Salaat.

Ruling: It is a communal obligation. (Far<u>d</u> Kifaayah). It has to be done by as many Muslims, as can make it.

When: It can be done any time during the day or night.

Where: The Jinaazah <u>S</u>alaat can be done in a mosque or any hall. It also can be done in the mu<u>s</u>al-laa or in a graveyard before the deceased is buried.

Who: Every free, sane, adult Muslim; male or female.

Conditions: ❶ The same conditions of any <u>S</u>alaat.

Description:

❶ The deceased should be placed between the imaam and Qiblah.

❷ The imaam stands opposite the head of a male, but stands in the middle of a female.

❸ The Jinaazah <u>S</u>alaat includes 4 takbiirahs.

❹ It is performed only in the standing position.

❺ It is performed by men and women.

❻ It is performed collectively or individually.

❼ After the first takbiirah, the Fati<u>h</u>ah should be recited.

❽ After the 2nd takbiirah, the salutation is given to the Messenger, as it is offered in (the 2nd half of tashah-hud).

❾ After the 3rd takbiirah, supplications are made for the deceased person. There are some supplications to be offered. One such du'aaˆ is the following:

"O Allah! Forgive our living and our dead, those present and those absent, our young and our old, our males and our females. O Allah, whom amongst us You keep alive, then let such a life be with Islam, and whom amongst us You take unto Yourself, then let such a death be with faith. O Allah, do not deprive us of his reward, and do not let us stray after him." **Ibn Majah & A<u>h</u>mad**

❿ After the 4th takbiirah, he makes du'aaˆ. Followed by tasliim (to the right). Tasliim to the right and left is also acceptable.

Recommended Issues:

❶ People are recommended to stand in 3 or more rows (both men and women).

❷ If one misses takbiirahs, one can make them up when the imaam finishes tasliim. But, if the funeral is taken to the grave immediately and one wishes to follow it, one can do tasliim with the imaam.

❸ The deceased benefits from this <u>S</u>alaat. The Messenger (pbuh) said: *"If 40 Muslims, who do not have shirk perform <u>S</u>alaat for the deceased, Allah will forgive the deceased."* **Muslim**

Salaat Jinaazah صَلاةُ الْجِنَازَةِ

Evidence:

❶ Ibn 'Ab-baas narrated that he performed Jinaazah Salaat and recited the Fatihah. Then he said: *"This is to let you know that it is the sun-nah."* **Al-Bukhari**

❷ Anas Ibn Malik performed Jinaazah Salaat for a deceased male. He stood in front of his head. Then when he finished, a deceased female was brought to him. At that time, he directed himself to the middle of the Jinaazah. Then he said: *"That is what the Messenger of Allah used to do."*
Ahmad, Ibn Majah, At-Termizi, and Abu Dawuud.

Questions & Answers

Q Is it permissible for one to raise the hands in every takbiirah?

A Yes, it has been done by Abdullah Ibn 'Umar and other companions (ra).

Q If one arrives after the imaam has finished the 2 takbiirahs of the Jinaazah Salaat, what can one do?

A One does the 3rd takbiirah exactly as the imaam and then du'aai for the deceased. Then, if the imaam makes tasliim, one can continue to make up what was missed exactly as the imaam did.

Q If the Jinaazah is taken away, should one continue to make up the missed part?

A One has an option to continue or stop.

Q Should one do one or two tasliimahs at the end of the Salaat?

A One has the option to do one or two tasliimahs. However, it is better to do it once, as the Messenger of Allah did.

Q Is wuduuˆ required for the Jinaazah Salaat?

A Yes.

Q What is the reward for those who attend the Jinaazah Salaat?

A The Messenger (pbuh) said: "Whoever witnesses a Jinaazah until the Salaat is over, would get a qiiraat* of good deeds; and whoever witnesses the burial would get two qiiraats.

Common Errors:

❶ Performing Jinaazah Salaat without wuduuˆ.

❷ Celebrating the 40th night after the death of a person.

❸ Wearing black clothes as a sign of mourning.

❹ Gathering in the house of the deceased person for 3 days.

Golden Tip:

❶ The Messenger (pbuh) taught us that if 40 people have no shirk in their hearts offer Jinaazah Salaat, Allah will forgive the deceased person. In these critical moments, you should be there. Hopefully, Allah might forgive the deceased person.

Imaam
The imaam raises his voice in takbiirs.

Maˆmuum
The maˆmuum does not.

Individual
The individual does not.

Males & Females
No difference.

*A qiiraat is defined by the prophet (pbuh) to be equivalent to mount Uhud)

Definition: It is basically a supplication that is performed after a Salaat when one seeks to make a decision or select from permissible options. It can also be performed after a non-obligatory Salaats.

Ruling: It is recommended.

When: It can be done at any time, day or night, at times of necessity, and even at usually prohibited times such as after 'Asr.

Where: It can be done anywhere like an obligatory Salaat.

Who: It can be done by any, sane, adult Muslim.

Conditions: It is done individually, not collectively.

Description: After doing a two- rak'ah Salaat one should say the following supplication:

Supplication:

"O Allah! I consult You as You are the All-Knowing and I appeal to You to give me power as You are Omnipotent. I ask You for Your great favor, for You have power and I do not, and You know all matters but I do not. O Allah, if You know that this issue (name it) is good for me in my religion, my current life, and for my Afterlife, facilitate it for me. But, if you know that this issue (name it) is not good for me in my religion, my current life and Afterlife, then keep it away from me and keep me away from it, and choose the best for me wherever it is and please me with it."

اللَّهُمَّ أَسْتَخِيرُكَ بِعِلْمِكَ وَأَسْتَقْدِرُكَ بِقُدْرَتِكَ وَأَسْأَلُكَ مِنْ فَضْلِكَ العَظِيمِ فَإِنَّكَ تَقْدِرُ ولا أَقْدِرُ ، وَتَعْلَمُ وَلا أَعْلَمُ اللَّهُمَّ إِنْ كُنْتَ تَعْلَمُ أَنَّ هَذَا الأَمْرَ خَيْرٌ لِي فِي دِينِي وَمَعَاشِي وَعَاقِبَةِ أَمْرِي فاقْدِرْهُ لِي وَيَسِّرْهُ لِي ثُمَّ بَارِكْ لِي فِيهِ . وَإِنْ كُنْتَ تَعْلَمُ أَنَّ هَذا الأَمْرَ شَرٌّ لِي فِي دِينِي وَمَعَاشِي وَعَاقِبَةِ أَمْرِي فاصْرِفْهُ عَنِّي واصْرِفْنِي عَنْهُ. واقْدِرْ لِي الخَيْرَ حَيْثُ كَانَ . ثُمَّ أَرْضِنِي بِهِ.

Recommended Issues:

❶ It is recommended to say the supplication after finishing the Salaat itself.

❷ There is no specific number of times.

❸ In this Salaat, one can also read any suurah. There is nothing specific.

Evidence:

❶ Jaabir (ra) narrated that the Messenger of Allah (pbuh) said: *"Whenever a person intends to do anything, he must pray two rak'ahs other than the obligatory Salaat. Then, he should recite the (above mentioned du'aaˆ)."* **Al-Bukhari**

Questions & Answers

Q1 What is the benefit of Salaatu-l-istikhaarah?

A It does not necessarily cause one's hesitation to disappear. The decision made, however, would be the best for that person.

Q2 What do I expect after doing Salaatu-l-istikhaarah?

A After Salaat, if you have a clear inclination towards a particular option, do it. But if you are still hesitant select the option that you think is better.

Q3 Is it permissible to do Salaatu-l-istikhaarah more than once?

A Yes, it is.

Q4 How many times can I redo it?

A Unlimited. Whenever you want to make a decision, offer the Salaat (du'aaˆ).

Q5 For what issues can I offer Salaatu-l-istikhaarah?

A You can offer it for any issue except two:

a. When the issue is an obligation to be performed anyway such as performing Hajj.

b. When the issue is a forbidden matter to be avoided anyway such as mortgage.

Common Errors:

❶ Some people expect to see a dream to guide them make their selection.

❷ Some people think that making Salaatu-l-istikhaarah replaces consulting people.

Golden Tip:

❶ This Salaat manifests true reliance upon Allah. Performing Salaatu-l-istikhaarah shows how much people are in need for their Lord to guide him. So, do not miss this free Divine consultation.

Imaam
Maˆmuum
Individual

No difference as this Salaat is always done individually.

Males & Females

No difference.

A Washing Both Hands

B Cleaning the Mouth

C Inhaling Water through Nose

D Washing the Face

E Washing Both Arms

F Wiping the Head

G Wiping the Ears

H Washing Both Feet

I Facing the Qiblah

J Takbiirat al-Ihram

K Reciting the Qur'an

L Making Rukuu'

M Rising from Rukuu'

N Making 1st Sujuud

O Sitting after 1st Sujuud

P Making 2nd Sujuud

Q Rising from Sujuud

R Beginning 2nd Rak'ah

S Making Rukuu'

T Rising from Rukuu'

U Making 1st Sujuud

V Sitting after 1st Sujuud

W Making 2nd Sujuud

X Sitting for Tashah-hud

Y Sitting for Last Tashah-hud

Z Making Tasliim

Section Five
Appendices

Types of Sujuud

Name	1 Sujuud of <u>S</u>alaat	2 Sujuud of Forgetting	3 Sujuud of Recitation	4 Sujuud of Thanks
Definition	It is a regular sujuud which one does in <u>S</u>alaat after rukuu'.	It is a sujuud which one does at the end of <u>S</u>alaats to make up for the error made during <u>S</u>alaat.	It is a sujuud which one does when coming across an aayah that requires a sajdah whether during <u>S</u>alaat or normal reading of the Qur'an.	It is a sujuud which one does to thank Allah for any thing (i.e. good news).
Description	One prostrates and places one's head on the ground saying (Subhaana rab-biya-l-A'laa).	It requires 2 sajdahs which look like the regular sujuud of obligatory <u>S</u>alaats. See details below.	It is just one sajdah, in which one says: سَجَدَ وَجْهِيَ لِلَّذِي خَلَقَهُ وَشَقَّ سَمْعَهُ وَبَصَرَهُ بِحَوْلِهِ وَقُوَّتِهِ فَتَبَارَكَ اللهُ أَحْسَنُ الْخَالِقِينَ Meaning: "My face prostrated to the One who created it; the one who slit its hearing and its seeing with His might & power. So, glory be to Allah, the best of the Creators"	It is one sajdah, in which one says: سُبْحانَ رَبِّيَ الأعْلى (Subhaana rab-biya-l-A'laa). Then one can say any du'aaˆ of sujuud.

Sujuud of Forgetting سُجُودُ السَّهْوِ

A Addition	**B** Omission	**C** Doubt
If one adds a rukn (intentionally) one's <u>S</u>alaat becomes invalid. But if he add a rukn (inadvertently), one's <u>S</u>alaat is valid as long as one rectifies the error by doing sujuud as-sahwu after tasliim.	But if one omits a rukn, there are 2 cases: a) If one forgets a rukn then remembers it before reaching the same pillar in the following rak'at, one should go back and do the missed rukn and whatever should follow it. b) If one remembers while doing the same rukn in the following rak'at, one should not go back to do the previous rukn. Rather, one should continue the <u>S</u>alaat and then add another rak'at instead of the one in which the rukn was forgotten. In these 2 cases, one has to make sujuud of forgetting after tasliim.	If one is in doubt and is ambivalent between addition and omission, i.e. whether he prayed 3or 4 rak'ahs, there are 2 cases: a) If one is totally uncertain, one assumes to have done the lower number of rak'ahs. In this case one does sujuud before tasliim. b) If one leans to a certain number of rakats thinking that to be the most likely, one continues the <u>S</u>alaat based on this tendency. i.e. If one thinks that one most likely did 3 rak'ahs, one should do a 4th one. In this case the sujuud should be after the tasliim.

أَنْوَاعُ السُّجُودِ

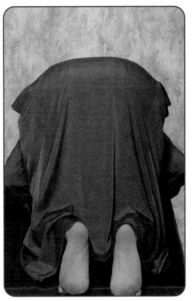

Questions & Answers

 1 Is sujuud of the recitation Waajib?

A No, it is not.'Umar ibn al-Khattab (ra) recited suurat an-Nahl on a Friday and did this sujuud, but, on another Friday, he recited the same suurah without doing this sujuud.
(see the supplication of sujuud of recitation under supplications)

 2 While I was praying with the imam, I forgot to say the tashahhud, what should I do?

A You are not required to do sujuud as-sahwu because you are a maˆmuum.

 3 I missed one rak'at with the imam. Then, when I was making up the missed rak'ah after the imam did tasliim, I forgot a waajib. What should I do?

A Do 2 sajdahs before tasliim.

 4 What is the ruling on one who commits more than one sahwu in one Salaat?

A You are not required to do sujuud sahwu for every sahwu. One sujuud as-sahwu is enough.

 5 How is the sujuud of recitation performed?

A Do takbiir, prostrate and say tasbiih, then rise from sujuud and do not do any tasliim.

 6 Can I make sujud ash-shukr during any of the obligatory or voluntary Salaats?

A No. It is not permissible.

 7 If I am listening attentively to the recitation of the Qur'an by one who comes across an aayah requiring sujuud. What should I do?

A If the reader does sujuud, you do sujuud. Otherwise, you are not supposed to do it.

A Golden Tip

1 Sujuud of Thanks is a sign to show gratitude to Almighty God for his blessings and bounties. So, show gratitude to God whenever you realize his great bounties.

Males
No difference.

Females
No difference.

Salaat in Brief
Number of Rak'ahs & Manner of Recitation

	No. of Rak'ahs	What is Recited		Manner of Recitation		
		Al-Fati<u>h</u>ah	Qur'an	Imaam	Ma^muum	Individual
Fajr 2 rak'ahs	1	*	Any Chapter(s)	Audible	Silent	Optional
	2	*	Any Chapter(s)	Audible	Silent	Optional
Żuhr 4 rak'ahs	1	*	Any Chapter(s)	Silent	Silent	Silent
	2	*	Any Chapter(s)	Silent	Silent	Silent
	3	*	N/A	Silent	Silent	Silent
	4	*	N/A	Silent	Silent	Silent
'Asr 4 rak'ahs	1	*	Any Chapter(s)	Silent	Silent	Silent
	2	*	Any Chapter(s)	Silent	Silent	Silent
	3	*	N/A	Silent	Silent	Silent
	4	*	N/A	Silent	Silent	Silent
Maghrib 3 rak'ahs	1	*	Any Chapter(s)	Audible	Silent	Optional
	2	*	Any Chapter(s)	Audible	Silent	Optional
	3	*	N/A	Silent	Silent	Silent
'Ishaa 4 rak'ahs	1	*	Any Chapter(s)	Audible	Silent	Optional
	2	*	Any Chapter(s)	Audible	Silent	Optional
	3	*	N/A	Silent	Silent	Silent
	4	*	N/A	Silent	Silent	Silent

Optional means: *according to the majority of scholars, the individual has the option to recite the Fati<u>h</u>ah and the Qur'an audibly or silently.*

Glossary

Aayah/ayah Sign/evidence	آيَةٌ	A verse from the Holy Qur'an. In fact, every verse in the Qur'an is a sign or a proof that it is from the Almighty Allah.
Azaan Call for Salaat	أَذانٌ	It is the call for Salaat. It represents the beginning of the legal time for the Salaat.
Basmalah In the name of Allah	بَسْمَلَةٌ	Saying in the name of Allah, the most Merciful, and the most Compassionate.
Du'aaˆ Supplication	دُعاءٌ	It is any supplication or request addressed to Allah.
Eiid (Eid) Feast/ Celebration	عِيدٌ	It is the Salaat that is performed on the occasion of the two Islamic feasts, Eiidul Fitri, and Eiidul- Adhaa.
Fard 'ayn Obligation for every individual	فَرْضُ عَيْنٍ	It is an obligatory Salaat for every free, adult, sane Muslim. It is not enough to be done by some Muslims only. For example, the five daily Salaats are obligatory for every Muslim.
Fard Kifaayah Communal Obligation	فَرْضُ كِفايَةٍ	It is a communal obligation. It is enough to be done by some. For example, Jinazah Salaat is not obligatory for every Muslim but it has to be done by some Muslims.
Fatwaa Ruling (ijtihad)	فَتْوى	It is a scholarly ruling on a religious issue.
Fiqh Jurisprudence	فِقْهٌ	The understanding and application of Sharii'ah Law from its sources.
Ghusl Taking a shower	غُسْلٌ	It is the state of cleaning one's body by washing all parts of the body especially after a sexual intercourse or a menstruation period or after the end of menses that follows birth.
Hadiith/Hadith Sayings	حَدِيثٌ	It refers to the sayings, the traditions, and the approvals of acts by the Messenger of Allah Muhammad (peace be unto him).
Halaal Lawful	حَلالٌ	It is everything, actions and sayings, which is deemed legal by the Sharii'ah Law.
Haraam Unlawful	حَرامٌ	It is everything, actions and sayings, which is deemed illegal by the Sharii'ah Law.
Hayd Menstruation	حَيْضٌ	It is the menstruation blood of women.
Hinnah Herbal dye	حِنَّةٌ	It is an herbal dye that is used for hands, feet, and hair.

Glossary

Iftiraash A certain sitting	اِفْتِراشٌ	It is a position in Salaat during the 1st tashahhud where the top of the left foot touches the ground while the right foot remains upright. The toes face the Qiblah.
Imaam Leader/guide	إِمامٌ	In general, he is the person who leads others. In particular, it refers to the person who leads people in the Salaat.
Iqaamah Establishing	إِقامَةٌ	It is the call informing people to stand up in lines for the Salaat.
'Ishaa Night Salaat	عِشاءُ	It is the last Salaat of the day. It consists of four rak'ahs (units).
Isti'aazah Taking refuge	اِسْتِعاذَةٌ	Saying "A'uuzu bil-laahi mina-sh-shaytaani-r-rajiim.", which means I take refuge with Allah from Satan.
Istikhaarah Consultation	اِسْتِخارَةٌ	It is a non-obligatory Salaat performed by one seeking Allah's help in making a lawful decision.
Istinshaaq Inhaling water	اِسْتِنْشاق	It is the act of inhaling water into one's nose (nostrils) the process of wuduuˆ (ablution).
Istisqaaˆ Seeking rain	اِسْتِسْقاءُ	It is a Salaat performed at times of droughts asking Allah for rain.
Jam' Combining or bringing together	جَمْعُ	It refers to the permissibility of combining two Salaats at a time. There are some situations which make it permissible to pray zuhr &'asr or maghrib & 'Ishaaˆ Salaats together in the Masjid. Such situations can traveling, being ill, and in times of hardships such as rain, snow, etc.
Jinaazah Funeral	جِنازَةٌ	It is the Salaat offered for the deceased.
Jumu'ah (Salaat) Friday prayer	جُمُعَةٌ	It refers to the two rak'ats of congregational Salaat, which is performed every Friday.
Ka'bah Ka'bah	كَعْبَةٌ	It is the first shrine ever built for worshipping Allah. It is a cubic building covered by black clothes. It is in Makkah inside al-masjid al-Haraam.
Khawf Salaat Fear prayer	خَوْفُ (صَلاة)	It is the Salaat, performed at times of danger and threat.
Khuffayn Two sandals	خُفَّيْن	It is the heelless shoes, sandals (socks) which are used in Salaat. In the state of wuduuˆ, one can wipe them with water.
Khusuuf (Salaat) Eclipse prayer	خُسُوفُ	It is the Salaat performed when there is a lunar or a solar eclipse.

Glossary

Ma^muum A follower	مَأمُومٌ	Is the person who is lead in a Ṣalaat .i.e. who follows the leader in Ṣalaat.
Madmadah Rinsing the mouth	مَضْمَضَةٌ	It is the act of rinsing one's mouth by water during the process of wuduu^ (ablution).
Maghrib (Ṣalaat) Sunset Ṣalaat	مَغْرِبٌ	It is the sunset Ṣalaat which consists of three rak'ahs (units).
Mut-tafaqun 'alayhi Agreed Upon	مُتَّفَقٌ عَلَيهِ	It is a prophetic hadiith that had been agreed upon by Imaam Muslim and Imaam al- Bukhari. This means that the ḥadiith is very authentic.
Nabiyy A Prophet	نَبِيٌّ	A prophet or a messenger of Allah.
Nafl Voluntary prayer	نَفْلٌ	It means extra. In Islamic context it means the sun-nah, which is less emphasized than the stressed sun-nah.
Najaasah Impurity	نَجاسَةٌ	All types of filth such as dead animals, dead bodies, blood, pig's meat, vomit, sperm, urine, and stool etc.
Qaṣr (Ṣalaat) Shortening	قَصْر (صَلاة)	It refers to the shortening of the four rak'at Ṣalaats to only two. Zuhr, 'Asr, and 'Ishaa^ can be shortened to two rak'ahs instead of four. This is a privilege given to travelers.
Qiblah Direction	قِبْلَةٌ	It is the direction which Muslims face during the Ṣalaat. It is Makkah in Saudi Arabia.
Qunuut Supplication in Ṣalaat	قُنُوتٍ	A supplication which said particularly in the witr Ṣalaat; before or after the rukuu' of the last rak'at and can be done all the year round. However, Fajr qunuut is recommended only at times of calamities.
Rak'ah Unit	رَكْعَةٌ	The basic cycle (unit) of Ṣalaat, which includes standing, bowing, and prostration.
Rasuul Messenger	رَسُولٌ	It refers to the messenger of Allah; i.e. Muhammad (peace be unto him).
Rukn Pillar	رُكْنٌ	The sayings and acts of the Messenger of Allah (pbuh) which if neglected intentionally, the Ṣalaat becomes invalid; not accepted and must be redone.
Rukuu' Bowing down	رُكُوعٌ	The state of bowing down in the Ṣalaat. It shows respect, love, and submission to the Almighty Allah. It should be done only for Him.
Ṣalaat Supplication/ prayer	صَلاةٌ	As a ritual, it is a set of acts and sayings which begins with a specific intention and takbiir, and it ends with tasliim". It refers to both the obligatory and the non-obligatory Ṣalaats.

Glossary

Sujuud Prostration	سُجُودٌ	The state of putting one's head on the ground while performing Salaats. In this position one is the closest to the Almighty Allah.
Sujuud As-sahwu Prostration of Forgetting	سُجُودُ السَّهْوِ	It is the sujuud made whenever one forgets to do an act in the Salaat.
Sujuud Ash-shukr Prostration for thanks	سُجُودُ الشُّكْرِ	It is the sujuud made whenever one wants to offer thankfulness to Allah. It can be made at anytime.
Sujuud At-tilaawah Prostration of recitation	سُجُودُ التِّلاوَةِ	It is the sujuud made during the recitation of the Qur'an. There are specific places in the Qur'an that require the person to prostrate.
Sun-nah Way, Tradition	سُنَّةٌ	The sayings and acts of the Messenger of Allah (pbuh) which are not essential to the Salaat. However, skipping these sunans means less rewards.
Sun-nah Mu^ak-kadah Stressed Sun-nah	سُنَّةٌ مُؤَكَّدَةٌ	It is the saying or the act of the Messenger of Allah (pbuh) which he stressed frequently, stressed during his life.
Sun-nah Raatibah Most stressed	سُنَّةٌ رَاتِبَةٌ	It is the saying or the act of the Messenger of Allah (pbuh) which he never neglected even in his travel such as the sun-nah of Fajr and the sun-nah of Witr.
Sutrah A Barrier	سُتْرَةٌ	An object that is placed in the place of sujuud, to separate between the one who prays and any person or thing that might pass by in front of him such as (a chair, a piece of wood, or a line).
Taarik as-Salaat Salaat neglector	تَارِكُ الصَّلاةِ	This term refers to one who intentionally neglects the Salaat for no legitimate excuse.
Tahliil Saying "there is no deity but Allah."	تَهْلِيلٌ	It means saying "There is no deity worthy of worship except Allah."
Tahmiid Praising Allah	تَحْمِيدٌ	It means saying "Praise be to Allah."

Glossary

Takbiir Saying "Allahu akbar"	تَكْبِيرٌ	It means saying Allaahu akbar which means Allah is Greater. This is a means magnifying and glorifying the Almighty Allah.
Takbiiratul-Ihraam Saying "Allahu akbar"	تَكْبِيرَةُ الإِحْرَامِ	The 1st time one says Allaahu akbar at the beginning of the Salaat. It is the signal after which all acts and sayings other than those of the Salaat become unlawful during the Salaat.
Takhliil Running water between the fingers	تَخْلِيلٌ	It is the process of running the water through the fingers or the toes to make sure that the water touches every spot of the hands or the feet.
Tasbiih Glorifying Allah	تَسْبِيحٌ	It is the saying of (subhana Allah) Glory be to Allah. Here, it refers to the tasbiih usually said after every Salaat. It can, however, be said anytime.
Tasliim Wishing Peace	تَسْلِيمٌ	It basically means saying "May peace be unto you" at the end of the Salaat. It is also used as the daily greetings among Muslims which means bidding each other peace and safety.
Tawa-rruk Sitting on left thigh	تَوَرُّكٌ	It is a form of sitting during tashahhud in 4 rak'at Salaats. In this position, one sits on the left thigh and places the left leg under the right leg. The right foot is placed in an upright position with its toes facing the Qiblah.
Tayam-mum Dry Ablution	تَيَمُّمٌ	It is a substitution for wuduuˆ. It is the use of pure earth or sand to rub ones face and hands as a substitute for water in such cases such as sickness or the lack of water.
Waajib Obligatory	وَاجِبٌ	The sayings and acts of the Messenger of Allah (Pbuh) which, if neglected intentionally or forgotten then remembered, can be made up by doing sujuud as- sahwi.
Witr Odd number (for night Salaat)	وِتْرٌ	It refers to the last Salaat at night consisting of and odd number of rak'ahs; one, three, five, etc.
Wuduuˆ Ablution	وُضُوءٌ	It is the state of ablution that requires washing or wiping the hands, mouth, nose, face, head, ears, arms, and feet as described in the chapter of wuduuˆ.

References

Author	Name of Reference	Publisher	Year
Al-'Adawi, Mustapha	Times of Salaats In Arabic	Al-Bayan Library, Taif, KSA.	1988
Al-Albaani, M. Naasir	The Prophet's Salaat Described	Al-Haneef Publications, UK.	1990
Ash-shafi'y, Mohammad	Musnad Ash-shafi'y	Dar Al-Fikr, Beirut, Lebanon	0000
Al-Asqalani, Ibn Hajar	Attainment of the Objectives	Dar usSalam Publications, Riyadh, KSA	1996
Al-Qazwinii, Abu Abdullah	Sunan Ibn Majah	Dar Al-Fikr, Beirut, Lebanon	0000
Al-Bukhari, Abu Abdullah	Al-Jami' As-sahiih	Salafi Press, Cairo, Egypt	1400 H
Al-Khateeb, Jalaal	Teaching Salaats for Muslim Men	I.I.F.S.O. Riyadh	1997
Al-Jawziyyah, Ibn Qayyem	The Book of Salat & The Ruling of the One Who Abandons it (In Arabic)	The Islamic Office, Beirut Lebanon	1985
Al-Marawazi, M.	Glorifying the Status of Salaat	Maktabat Ad-Dar, Madinah, USA	0000
Al-Qahtani, Sa'eed	Fortification of the Muslim	Minstry of Islamic Affairs Riyadh, KSA	1998
Al- Uthaimiin, M.	Sifat Als-Salaat	Maktab-at Al-Sun-nah	1995
Al- Uthaimiin, M.	Speeches in Cleanliness and Salaats	Dar Al-Watan, Riyadh, KSA	1990
Al-Uthaimiin, M.	Questions & Answers about Salat Al-Eiids	IIASA, VA. USA	0000
American Trust Publications	Friday Salaat	American Trust Publications, IN	0000
At-Termizi, Abu Abdullah	Salaat and it Objectives	Dar Ihya^ Al-'Ulum, Beirut, Lebanon	1986
At-Termizi, Abu Abdullah	Sunan At-Termizi	The Islamic Library, Istanbul, Turkey	0000
Darussalam Research Division	Salaat for Beginners	Dar us-Salam Publications, Riyadh, KSA	2000
Dept. of Education	Tawheed & Fiqh (3rd grade) (In Arabic)	Dept of Ed. KSA	1998
Dept. of Education	Tawheed & Fiqh (4th grade) (In Arabic)	Dept of Ed. KSA	1998
Dept. of Education	Tawheed & Fiqh (5th grade) (In Arabic)	Dept of Ed. KSA	1998
Fazlul Karim, Maulana	Imam Gazaali's Ihya 'Ulum-Id-Din	Kitab Bhavan, New Delhi, India	1982

References

Author	Name of Reference	Publisher	Year
Haneef, Suzanne	What Everyone Should Know About Islam and Muslims	Kazi Publications. IL, USA	1996
Hanbal, Ahmad	Al-Musnad	The Islamic Office, Amman	0000
Hasan, Suhaib	Why Do We Pray?	Darussalam Riyadh	1996
Ibn Baz, A.	Salat According to the manners of Prophet Muhammad	Darussalam, NY. USA	1995
Ibn Baz, A.	Prophet Manner of Performing Salaat	Cooperative Office Riyadh, KSA	1992
Millat Book Centre	The Muslim Salaat	Millat Book Centre	0000
Muslim, Abu Al-Hussain	Sahih Muslim	The Islamic Library, Istanbul, Turkey	0000
Muslim Converts' Ass. of Singapore	Let's Pray (Male)	Pustaka national Pte. Ltd. Singapore	1999
Muslim Converts' Ass. of Singapore	Let's Pray (Female)	Pustaka National Pte. Ltd. Singapore	1999
Nograles, Jameel	Al-Wudhuuˆ wa as-Salaah	Cooperative Office for Call & Guidance, Riyadh	0000
Quraishi, Abdul Basit	The Manner of Performing Salaats	Foreigners Guidance Center, Gassim, KSA	1991
Rifa'I, Mohamed	Tuntunan Salaat Lenghap	Toha Putra, Semarang, Indonesia	0000
Sabiq, Sayed	Fiqh Al-Sun-nah	Dar Al-Qalam, Lebanon	1982
Sakr, Ahmad H.	Prostration (Sujuud)	Found. Of Islamic Knowledge, Il. USA	1997
Saqib, M. A. K.	A Guide to Salaat in Islam	Intern. Islamic Pub. House, Riyadh	1997
Shad, Abdur Rehaman	The Prescribed Islamic Salaats	Kazi Publications, Lahore, Pakistan	1979
Sulaiman, Abu Dawuud	Sunnan Abi Dawuud	Dar Al-Hadiith, India	1393 H
Ulayyan, Shawkat	The Total Salaats in Islam (In Arabic)	Media Department, Riyadh, KSA	1990
Ya'quub, M. Hussein	Why Do not You Pray (Audio Tape) (In Arabic)	Cairo, Egypt	1997
Zarabozo, Jamaal al-Din	The Friday Salaat	IANA, Ann Arbor, MI, USA	1998

0000 = No data was mentioned in the book

Index

Index

Index

Publications by the Author

No.	Name	Type	Language
1	Salaat: The Islamic Prayer from A to Z	Book w/ CD	English
2	Hajj & Umrah from A to Z	Book	English
3	Seerah for All: Educational Perspective	Book	Arabic & Eng.
4	Arabic: A Bridge to Islamic Culture (Volume I)	Book w/ CD	Arabic & Eng.
5	Arabic: A Bridge to Islamic Culture (Volume II)	Book w/ CD	Arabic & Eng.
6	Arabic: A Bridge to Islamic Culture (Volume III)	Book w/ CD	Arabic
7	Arabic: A Bridge to Islamic Culture (Volume IV)	Book w/ CD	Arabic
8	Arabic: A Bridge to Islamic Culture (Student's & Teacher's Guide)	Book	Arabic & Eng.
9	The Religion of Islam	Mac CD	English
10	Arabic for Children 4 Volumes (Co-authored)	Book	English
11	Islam in Brief	Power Point Presentation	English
12	The Purpose of Life	Audio CD	English
13	Arrogance	Audio CD	English
14	How we love the Prophet (Peace be unto him)	Audio CD	English
15	Why we love the Prophet (Peace be unto him)	Audio CD	English
16	The Best Generation	Audio CD	English
17	Perfection	Audio CD	English
18	Insights in the Qur'an	Audio CD	Arabic
19	Qualities of Believers (Muttaqeen)	Audio CD	English
20	How the Learn Qur'anic Arabic (2 CDs)	Audio CDs	English
21	Obstacles on the Path of Change	Audio CD	English
22	How to Gain Khushu' in Salaat	Audio CD	English
23	Maximizing Your Benefits from the Qur'an	Audio CD	English
24	A Love Story	Audio CD	English
25	Learn Arabic by Yourself	Audio CD	English
26	Parents! Help Your Kids Learn Arabic	Audio CD	English
27	Arabic for Kids	Power Point Presentation	English
28	Arabic Lessons for Adults	Power Point Presentation	English
29	Oh ! My Worshippers (Slaves)	Audio CD	English
30	Fruits of Worship	Audio CD	English

Visit: www.islamfromAtoZ.com

About the Author

Dr. Mamdouh N. Mohamed

Adjunct Professor at George Mason University

*Associate Professor at
The American Open University,*

Virginia, USA.

He was born in Egypt 1949.

He obtained his first degree from 'Ain-Shams University in Egypt.

He received both his Masters and Ph. D. from George Mason University, USA.

He has worked as a teacher and teacher-trainer for more than 30 years.

He is an instructional technologist.

His most famous work is

Hajj & Umrah from A to Z.

He co-authored a 4-volume textbook for children

Arabic for Children

He is a developer of some educational software

Mission Survival
&
The Religion of Islam

He is a co-founder of 5 educational institutions worldwide.
He held a number of training courses in many countries.
He developed a five-volume textbook for teaching Arabic to non-Arabs;

Arabic: A Bridge to Islamic Culture

He received a patent in computer design from the USA Patent Office.
He held some teaching, research, and training jobs.
He worked in various international settings.

He is currently working as an educational advisor at American Open University.
He is a consultant for many other institutions.

He became an Associate Professor in March, 2003.

e-mail address:
info@arabicforeveryone.com

A	Washing Both Hands
B	Cleaning the Mouth
C	Inhaling Water through Nose
D	Washing the Face
E	Washing Both Arms
F	Wiping the Head
G	Wiping the Ears
H	Washing Both Feet
I	Facing the Qiblah
J	Takbiirat al-Ihram
K	Reciting the Qur'an
L	Making Rukuu'
M	Rising from Rukuu'
N	Making 1st Sujuud
O	Sitting after 1st Sujuud
P	Making 2nd Sujuud
Q	Rising from Sujuud
R	Beginning 2nd Rak'ah
S	Making Rukuu'
T	Rising from Rukuu'
U	Making 1st Sujuud
V	Sitting after 1st Sujuud
W	Making 2nd Sujuud
X	Sitting for Tashah-hud
Y	Sitting for Last Tashah-hud
Z	Making Tasliim

Salaat:
The Islamic Prayer
from
A to Z

Dr. Mamdouh N. Mohamed
Professorial Lecturer at Johns Hopkins University